I SLEPT WITH A MARRIED MAN

I Slept with a Married Man

Am I Still A Good Person?

JANELLE VILLIERS

SayThat Publishing

Gratitude

To my parents whose love and support are endless and for which there are not enough words to express my gratitude for.

To my former college roommate and friend for life, you were there at some of the most pivotal times in my life and for that I am deeply grateful.

To all those who read the first drafts of this book and helped me edit them. This wouldn't have happened without you. Thank you from the bottom of my heart.

To all of my friends, family and business partners whose continued encouragement for me put my story in print form got me through any times of doubt

To Dr. Goldstein (Dr. G), Thank you! Thank you! Thank you!

And finally, to YOU, kind reader, for deciding to read my story. Thank you!

If my story is able to resonate and/or help only one person then that would be enough.

I wrote this for you.

You are not alone.

CONTENTS

PART 1

"We have stories to tell. Stories that provide wisdom about the journey of life. What more have we to give one another than our 'truth' about our human adventure as honestly and as openly as we know how?" – Rabbi Saul Rubin

Chapter 1: I Slept with a married man – my rock bottom

Have you ever done something that you are ashamed of? Is there anything that you have done, kind reader, that you look back on and regret? Or something you did where you don't understand why you did it? Or why you wanted to do it?

I slept with a married man. And I'm coming clean about it, to you, kind reader.

I hate it. It's an act that had me constantly questioning: *Am I still a good person? Am I a good person at all?*

So where do I begin... I believe I have a set of morals, a moral compass. So why would someone with morals and a moral compass sleep with a married man? A man who, admittedly, was on the brink of divorce.

Why would I do that when I know what it feels like to be a married woman and have my husband cheat on me, multiple times, over many years?

I am surrounded by people, team members, family, colleagues, friends, business partners, who look at me and think I'm a good person. More importantly, I want to be thought of as a good person by these people. More than that, I will admit there is a large part of me that wants these people to think that I look, and that I am perfect. So, if I am perfect, I can protect myself from their judgment, criticism and potential hatred of who I really am. This need to look perfect to people, to look like a white sheet without any stains, is constant and overwhelming.

In order to keep up that appearance, I have to lie. It's a lie of omission. Of course, no one has ever asked me, outright, if I ever slept with a married man. And, obviously, I don't talk about it. If I don't talk about it or think about it, maybe I will forget it ever happened, and so will God and it will be like it never happened. And maybe, in the long run, when I'm 80 years old surrounded by my husband, children and grandchildren, it won't matter. I pray to God it won't!

For many years I thought I would keep this secret and take it to my grave.

An intelligent friend of mine, Todd, once said to me that "the person who does the "wrong" thing feels 10 times worse than the person that was wronged."

When he said these wise words, I immediately thought of this secret, that up until that moment I had told only one other person.

Could anyone still love me if they knew that I slept with a married man, that I had lied by omission by not telling anyone this aspect of myself? That I question and fear that there may be this dark part of me that exists? Could any man still love me knowing that? Could God still love me? Could I still love myself?

Because, Todd is right. I felt and still feel, as I write this, horrible about what I did.

And more so, how does this action confirm that I, in fact, am not worthy, not worthy of love, of good things happening to me, or of being happy?

And THERE it is! The constant thought I have had since I was a little girl, for as long as I can remember:

I am not worthy.

Shame is "I am a bad person." Whereas, guilt is: "I did a bad thing". Shame often also translates to "I am not lovable" or "I have no value" or "I am not enough" and also what I described above, "I am not worthy."

Have you ever had these feelings or beliefs, kind reader? Perhaps you can relate to feeling a sense of unworthiness, unlovableness, having no value? Is this a belief you have had for so long you don't even remember when it started? By sharing my story, we're going to talk about all of this .

At this time in my life, as I write, I have an undergraduate degree from an Ivy League University, I have earned a master's degree, I have the title of assistant director of a graduate program, I have my own successful Network marketing business as well as a YouTube channel, and I am a partner in another online service business. While dealing with all of these titles and adult responsibilities I've gotten lost in the idea that I need to constantly live a life of perfection.

But if I'm honest, I have felt the need to be perfect my entire life. That I could never do wrong, nor be seen doing anything wrong. Putting on a mask, I thought *people wouldn't have to get to know the real imperfect, unlovable me. It's better that they know the perfect version. That's the version of the person they will respect and value.*

In my youth I had friends who were not that perfect. They were "rebels" who did "bad" things or participated in "risky behavior". They had oral sex in middle school, sex in high school, and smoked weed. To be honest, a part of me wanted to be able to have the freedom to be able to do those things too. I was both appalled at their actions *and* admired them.

Is that too honest?

I was told not to tell you, kind reader, the reason why I slept with a married man in the beginning of this book. Many believe if I did that you would not read past the first few pages. I am to understand that in <u>this</u> day and age, with people's short attention spans and the freedom to make character judgments about someone after reading 140 characters, that you, kind reader, would do the same to me.

But I decided that I am going to go against that common way of thinking and instead tell you right now! I am going to share a story and reflection of how I got into this awful position and how this has changed me. Admittedly, my story will be a reflection of my memories of events and conversations. I recognize that the wording may not be exactly what was said in the years or months that have passed but that they are more likely to represent what I remember. What is most important is how these conversations impacted me. I hope that in sharing my journey with you, kind reader, that you will find my story real and authentic, comical, sometimes sad, always relatable and sprinkled with life lessons and a path towards healing. I believe my story can lead to what shame researcher and expert, Brene Brown, calls, "shame resilience".

So why did I sleep with a married man? I did it for many reasons. And if I am completely honest, which is the point of this book, one of the main reasons I did it was because I was curious. What would it be like to have sex with him? In addition, in that moment I was caught up in the fact that he found me attractive and wanted me sexually. Over ten years prior, before that moment I was told, mainly by my ex-husband, that I was not attractive, not sexy, he didn't desire me and I wasn't worth his time. And also, in that critical moment, I had the really crazy, though *fleeting*, thought of: *What if he IS the one for me?* And finally, another reason was the fact that the guy was dominating and forceful in his advances and flirting, which, admittedly, is a turn on for me, so also in that moment, I was very titillated.

And, ultimately, I gave into the carnal feelings and went with the flow.

Upon penetration, I immediately thought: *Nope! This is not a good thing to do. Having sex with him is not a good thing. He is married. Having sex with a married man is not good. I don't like doing this! I shouldn't be doing this.*

But it was too late... Thoughts continued to race through my brain: *I allowed it... If I allowed it... I can't say 'no' now, I already allowed it, right?! He won't listen to me say 'no' now. He was so forceful in his flirtations, I am sure he will ignore my 'no' and not believe I mean it. How can I get this to end as quickly as possible? What can I do so that this ends and he can leave?* So, I went through the motions... made the noises... hoping to God I sounded like I was being satisfied, the whole time thinking *I hope he doesn't know I'm faking and he is turned on enough to cum and this can be over...* and then it was.

And I felt ashamed and awful: *there it is... I had done it... this just proves it... I am not worthy to be loved. Would he even want to do this with me if he was not married? Probably not.* And now that it was over, if I wasn't attracted to him before, now, he was even more unattractive to me. Why? Because now, what I saw about myself as unattractive, unloveable and a bad person, I now saw in him. He was my mirror.

He left soon after, and I told myself, never again.

Until, we were alone two days later and I wanted to really prove to myself that I could handle being in the same room with him, he could apply the same pressure (dominating advances) but this time I would make it stop before it got that far and we wouldn't do it again. Scientists call this "restraint bias". The fact that humans think they have more willpower than they actually do. It's where we think we won't give into a temptation, so we take the risk of getting close, or allow ourselves to get too close to the thing we don't want to do, thinking we will be strong enough to stop it. But the thing is, using our will power takes a lot of energy. And we may be using that same energy throughout the day to show restraint. Fro example you don't eat one of the brownies in the break room at work. You don't tell your co-worker off when they're annoying you on the Zoom meeting. You made the decision to work out or pray or meditate in the morning even when you didn't feel like it. And then you get home and you yell at your partner and/or kids. Or you get home and eat an entire apple pie. You decide to flirt back with that person whom you know you should not be flirting with. Because the energy for restraint is now gone.

So there I was, utterly underestimating my restraint bias as he, once again, became dominant in his flirtation and I thought: *maybe that last time was just a fluke... maybe I didn't really feel like it was a bad idea.* But the minute I felt his penis, before he could even penetrate, I immediately felt the same way as last time and was even more disgusted with myself. I thought: *I can not do this again!* So, I came up with the only thing I could think of to say that I thought would stop him in mid action. I told him that "it hurt." I don't know why he bought that lame lie, but it worked! And we stopped.

Then he was just in my home and I thought: *How on earth can I get away from him and this situation without making him feel bad?*

Can you believe it, kind reader?! I wanted *him* to not feel bad.

I don't even remember what I said but eventually I was alone again and feeling awful.

Todd is right "when you do wrong, and you know it, you feel awful."

I am not sure if others who have slept with married men can say that they have felt awful, like I did. I have not done a poll, so this is a sample size of just one...me. But I am sure I can't be the only one. Right?

Alone in my apartment, I found myself asking a familiar question, internally. I was questioning my self-worth. *If you thought you weren't worthy of love, happiness, money or joy, before, you DEFINITELY are not worthy of it now.*

Our inner dialogue can sometimes say things to us that are worse than our strongest enemy.

But maybe you agree with my inner dialogue? I know at that time, I certainly did.

Which led to the need to lie, cover up, wear a mask. And never tell ANYONE that this ever happened, EVER.

Feeling that I was not a good person, I thought: *is there anything I can do to make up for being this kind of "bad person"? Probably never. Maybe if I cover it up by doing as many good things as possible. Maybe if I try to bring value to as many people as possible... maybe just maybe...*

So, I spent my time since then getting closer to God. Understanding that by believing in Jesus, my sins are forgiven. Reading the Bible, I understood that Noah got drunk, Abraham was old and lied, Leah was ugly, Sara was impatient, Jacob was a liar, Joseph was abused, Jonah ran from God, Miriam was a gossip, Job went bankrupt, Naomi was a widow, Gideon was afraid and insecure, Rahab was a prostitute, Elijah was burnt out and suicidal, Moses was a murderer who stuttered, David had an affair and was a murderer, Peter had a temper, Paul was a murderer, Mary worried about everything, The Samaritan woman who had five husbands and was living with a sixth man who was not her husband, Thomas was a doubter, and Lazarus was dead. It would seem that God not only forgives the ones who seem to have done the things that are unforgivable, but he also uses them to do some of his most profound works. In fact, He already knew my sin before I thought it, before I did it. This led me to a new stream of thought: *I should be alone, that all men, all humans should just stay away from me, because only God can love this sad girl of nothingness. This disgusting girl, full of shame and guilt.*

Ironically, in my Network Marketing business, I am surrounded by mentors, big thinkers, those who believe in personal development. They speak personal development. They live personal development. They hold themselves to a moral standard that I admire. They are always working on making themselves better. And you know the saying "you're the average of the top 5 people you surround yourself with." That goes for me as well. So, I am always working on making myself **better**. So, another thing I did after my shameful act, is that I dove headfirst into personal development, honestly hoping that some of it would rub off on me and I would become a better person.

Ultimately, I realized that I do believe that if God loves me and wants to give me abundance, that includes the right husband for me. But if God brought that man into my life in that moment of my deepest shame, would I have been ready for him? At that moment, I definitely did not believe I was. I understood that I needed to work on myself, to be the type of woman and wife that he would respect, admire, and cherish, one who can contribute to his goals, dreams and aspirations, be an asset to **everything** he does.

So, I forgave myself for all the bad things I have done in my past relationships.

I forgave myself.

Didn't I? If only it were as easy as saying it...

What I have come to learn, in my life, is that **everyone** is going through their own struggle. And I mean **everyone**. Dare I say, even *you*, my new friend and kind reader. Everyone is doing or has done something in their life that they wish they weren't doing or hadn't done.

There it is! That thing that you are thinking about right now as you read this, that you hope no one will ever know. Or that thing that you push into the very back of your mind and shut behind a door called "in my past." Or maybe that thing that you did that you overcame and already forgave yourself for. Whatever it is, we all have **that** something in our lives.

Brene Brown says that it is when we are vulnerable that we become strong. Well I hope that by sharing with you what I am most ashamed of, you, my new friend and kind reader, will see the strength in my shortcomings and mistakes, as I reveal myself, taking off one layer at a time... vulnerable... to your judgments, accusations and dislikes, as well as my own.

I am hoping that, maybe, in all the bad thoughts and actions I have done, that there is still something redeeming about my soul. That it might be possible that I am still a good person.

A good person who did bad things.

Chapter 2: I started off a good person... I think

Maybe you are thinking:

How did she get this way?

Can she be redeemed?

Could someone really be a good person and do bad things?

Is there anything she can do to make up for what she has done?

If *she* could find something she can do to be forgiven, to forgive herself, maybe I can do the same to forgive myself for the things that I have done?

Could that be possible?

None of us are born bad. None of us are born thinking: *how can I bring shame to all of the people around me, my family, friends and loved ones? How can I do something that could hurt another person? And how did I become a woman who could sleep with a married man?* So, how did I become someone who did that? Well, I confess that, like most people, I was born in a hospital. And then that's where the similarities end. Soon after birth I was officially adopted.

I knew that I was adopted since as early as I can remember. My mother has since told me that she and my dad would read children's books about adoption to me among other books like "Good Night Moon." However, I can't say that I remember those. I am certain they must have planted seeds in my subconscious because what I do remember that my mother told me, one specific evening, when I was no older than three. It's one of my earliest memories. My mom was in her bedroom sitting at the edge of her bed watching the news. I waddled in and crawled onto the bed and sat next to her. My feet reached the edge of the bed and I was swaying them side to side, like windshield wipers. When all of a sudden, I heard the news reporter mention something about "adoption." I remember I turned to my mother and asked, "Mommy, what does adoption mean?"

Bless my mother, she must have been thinking how she was going to tell me this for a very long time. And she responded with a brilliant answer!

"Well, adoption is when a mommy and daddy can't take care of their baby so they ask for other adults to be the mommy and daddy and take care of their baby." She paused, "You know you were adopted, Janelle, and me and your Dad love you very, very much." She hugged and squeezed me into her side while kissing me on my head.

"Oh, ok." I said as she released me. I jumped off the bed and waddled back into my room and played with my My-Little-Ponies. At 3 years-old, that's all I needed to know, I was adopted and my Mom & Dad loved me very, very much.

My parents had some difficulty having children before and after adopting me. They believed that this was God's way of telling them they should take in children who don't have (good) parents.

For that reason, they pursued foster care. For those of you not from the United States or who are not familiar, you might be wondering: *What's foster care?*

Foster care is a governmental program in America where, if parents who are not able to take care of their children (or mistreat their children), the State intervenes. The State places these children who are considered "at risk" with another set of pre-screened adults who will take care of them for a limited amount of time and money. In some jurisdictions the parents have some time to get their own lives together and then the child(ren) would return to them. However, as you can imagine, not every parent gets their act together, or changes their ways or creates a suitable environment. And then, of course, there are those biological parents who do not want their children to come back at all. When this happens, a child could live with one family and then another for weeks, months or years at a time. The constant switching of families can be quite traumatic. Ultimately, the best solution would be for the child(ren) to be adopted permanently into one family. Some kids stay in this system until they are 18 and can start to independently fend for themselves. Another fraction are adopted into a permanent family. To get an idea of this system, over-all, I suggest watching the movie: *Instant Family* starring Mark Wahlberg and Rose Byrne.

My parents received their first, of four foster children, a young eight year-old boy when I was twelve years old. This experience gave me some idea of what it was like to grow up with siblings. So, my new friend, if you questioned whether being a selfish only-child led to my selfish decisions as an adult, I can say that this childhood experience wiped out any "only-child" mindset I may have had. But I digress...

When I was fourteen years old I found out that I was getting "an older sister" as our next foster child. She was sixteen years old. I was so excited! So far, we had gotten two, younger boys. And at that age, little brothers are *so annoying!* I had secretly always wanted an older sister. Someone I could talk to, share feelings with, have fun with and do all the girly stuff. She would go on her first date before me, go to prom before me, so by the time I had to do those things it wouldn't be so new for my parents because they had already dealt with it once before. I remember cleaning out the bookshelves of the room that she was going to be staying in. Two side by side six feet tall, three feet wide bookcases, completely packed with stuff. My parents kept so many things: My first grade spelling quizzes, a book they used to read to me when I was four, another when I was five, other papers that had long been forgotten about. And then I saw it! A business size white envelope and on the top right corner of the envelope there was, what looked like, a stain from someone spilling red kool-aid on it. I cannot explain why, but in that moment, everything inside of my body told me that this envelope was going to have information about my birth parents. I quickly pulled the letter from out of the books it was sandwiched between, carefully opened it and unfolded a two page letter that was also stained with the red Kool-Aid. It was a letter from the adoption agency informing them of some information about my birth parents, "in case one day Janelle needs to know some medical information or history."

My birth parents were a fourteen year-old Puerto Rican girl and a seventeen year-old boy of St. Thomas origins. My birth mother, it said, was a dancer at the real-life performing arts high school in New York City (NYC) that the movie "Fame" was based on. *Funny... because I also love to dance.* It also said she was 5'3" at fourteen years old. *I have been 5'3" since I was 11 years old.* My biological father, the letter said was darker skinned and had a "prominent" forehead. *Maybe that's why I have a big forehead?!* The letter went on to say that my paternal grandmother was born with a heart murmur that went away after childhood and that both families were in fairly good health. The letter also commented that my birth mother had second thoughts about going through with the adoption after I was born but that her sister and mother (my grandmother and aunt) encouraged her to continue as it would be in my best interest.

Well, if I had ever wondered if my birth mother ever had any doubts, there was my answer! And if I wondered why she gave me up for adoption in the first place... there was that answer too! She was fourteen years old when she gave birth to me. I was fourteen years-old reading this letter.

There is no way at fourteen years old I could *ever* imagine having and taking care of a baby!

My adopted parents are light-skinned Jamaicans. I describe their skin tone because I believe that is the only physical feature we have in common. My adopted parents and I have often been told we look like each other. We always laughed with each other, a private joke, whenever someone said it. At first glance, some may say I appear ethnically ambiguous. In NYC, people, most often, immediately assume I'm from the Dominican Republic! Ultimately, I am Caribbean, no question about that!

My adopted parents are an absolute blessing! I do not know where I would be if I had been raised by my biological parents. But I'm confident I would not have received the same education. My parents grew up in a country that believed that "education" is the way you get out of your current life situation or stock in life. And so I was constantly and enthusiastically encouraged to do well in school. The way I looked and dressed were second to how I performed in school. I don't remember being told I was pretty or beautiful. I was consistently told that I was smart. I didn't realize, at that time, how I would internalize this simple difference in frequency between the two affirmations, and how it would play a role in shaping my self image.

In school I had bullies who told me "you are not as smart as you think you are" and "you're not pretty. You're ugly." They would tell me that I wasn't smart, but then begged me to teach or help them with their math homework. I can tell you I was smart enough to know that this didn't add up (pun intended!) I remember thinking: *How could I be dumb, but you ask me to help with (or sometimes do) your homework? Plus, my parents told me I was smart, so saying I was dumb must not be true.* On the other hand, *no ones frequently told me about my looks, except the bullies. So maybe that part was true. I must be smart but not pretty. Otherwise, wouldn't I have heard more often about how pretty I am by now?* Begrudgingly, I must admit that not being told I was pretty at a young age, more often, impacted my self-esteem as I grew up. My internal conversation often sounded like this in my head: *Why would any boy be interested in me? I am smart, but not that pretty. And boys only like pretty girls!*

While growing up, I had this sense that I wasn't doing enough in all areas including eating, sports and school work. I ate dinner but didn't eat fast enough, according to my father. I could play soccer ok, but never well enough against really good soccer players in my school. One time I got a very **hard**-earned "B" instead of an "A" in a history class. My parents told me they couldn't understand "why I wasn't trying hard enough." They shared that my grade was disappointing, and that there must have been something that they hadn't taught me, that would allow me to think that a B was acceptable. I interpreted and internalized this as them thinking *I* was a disappointment (not solely the grade) and that my best efforts were a disappointment. This particular conversation was probably worse than being grounded for a year. I felt the burden-heavy load of *being* a disappointment. For me, this was an example of how my best was not good enough and therefore, I was not good enough. At the end of high school, I ended up graduating in the top 10% of my class (Cum Laude) so one might say that their disappointment led me to work hard and ended up doing well in high school. So, it all worked out anyway, right?

Or, maybe the feeling of not being enough came solely from knowing I was adopted. This perpetuating idea, in the back of my mind, no matter how many times I was able to rationalize why a fourteen year-old with a baby should *definitely* give her child up for adoption. Yet, ultimately, I was unwanted from birth. Could I have internalized being given up to mean that I was not valuable enough or loveable enough from birth?

Or...could it be both?

Your guess is as good as mine.

Well... If you're still with me, kind reader, thank you! Thank you for being curious and wanting to know more, maybe even in this little time together you see a little of yourself in my story.

I am learning from my story as I continue to tell it in these pages! I realize now that I may have had shame-based thinking about my value and lovableness from childhood. Later, as an adult, this shame-based thinking was compounded by the poor view of myself as a sexual being and woman. There is a long list of things that I experienced that led me to believe that being sexual was wrong and that something is wrong with me "down there" that would make me undesirable. The best place to continue, I think, would be the day I became a woman.

Chapter 3: Am I the only one who has not had a normal relationship with her lady parts?

Officially, at eight years old, I had crossed a threshold from childhood to womanhood. For many, that may seem way too young. For my kind readers who identify as men, imagine having sex for the first time at ten years old or even eight! Or imagine having to tell a girl at 8 years old to be careful not to have sex with boys because, having her period means she can actually get pregnant... at eight years old! If it weren't my own story, I would even say it's too young for that type of transformative experience. I went through something that none of my female classmates had gone through which felt isolating. I was definitely alone. Of course, they talked dreamily of the day that they would get their periods too. But I was all alone in this maturation stage for a few more years of my life. To them I may have been cool because I entered womanhood BUT to me I was still the "other" and did not belong, oh, AND I had to be "careful around boys".

If to feel shame is to feel like you don't belong, alone and isolated.... add this early age of maturation to the bucket of shaming experiences I was subconsciously collecting.

When I was about eleven years-old I swam very competitively. But unlike many eleven year-olds I was already menstruating. So, the logical thing to do was to learn how to insert and use a tampon. However, I had problems inserting the tampon. So my mom thought it would be best to see a doctor to find out what was going on. I don't think either of us could have been prepared for the actual visit.

The exam room was small, the walls white, with the exam bed, which is in every OGBYN exam room, in the center, facing the left corner of the room. There were lights near that corner that I was not familiar with. Unlike my pediatrician visits, this room had no cool pictures, no cartoons, no real color, nothing that had any warmth at all. Everything about the room said "grown up." Once we were both inside, the nurse closed the door behind us and put the chart she was carrying on the small desk on the side of the room and gestured for us both to take a seat.

My mom and I sat in silence for a minute or two. Then she looked calmly at me and asked, "are you all right? Are you nervous?"

"No," I lied. She smiled down at me. "Ok, maybe a little?"

A few seconds later the door opened and a thin middle-aged White woman, wearing a white "doctor's lab coat" with short dark brown hair pulled back in a ponytail entered the room. She walked past us briskly, put the chart on the table and looked at us. A kind and warm smile spread across her face.

"Hello ladies, and how may I help you today? I hear we have a problem involving tampons?" Relieved I didn't have to hear my mother repeat the embarrassing problem that had become our story. I shook my head yes. My mother, answering for both of us, said, "Yes."

"Not a problem, I believe I can help with that." Internally, I expressed a huge sigh of relief. "I hear that you are a swimmer?" She looked at me, again with a smile on her face.

"Yes, I swim." I muttered shyly.

"That's great! And what is your best stroke?" At that, I perked up. She knew something about swimming! Most people outside of my swimming community didn't.

"Butterfly," I responded with a little more confidence. "I never even knew how to swim butterfly when I first joined the team and now it's my best stroke."

"Butterfly, wow! I am impressed! That is a very hard stroke to learn and to swim. Good for you! And how old were you when you first got your period?"

"I was 8 years old" I was gaining more confidence now.

"Oh! And how old are you now?"

"I am 11"

"Ok, great. Now I'm going to ask your mother to leave the room, so I can ask you a question alone, is that ok?" She looked at my mom, shaking her head yes, as if to say don't worry it's ok. *Oh! Wait, what's happening? I was just starting to get comfortable*, I thought. *What in the world could* she want to ask me that she couldn't ask me with my mother in the room? "Don't worry," she continued, "it will only be for a minute, I promise." Again, she looked at my mom, knowingly and said to her, "would that be ok with you, mom?"

"Oh, ok, yes that would be all right," my mom said and started to get up from her seat. She seemed relatively calm, so *I guess this couldn't be bad,* I thought. *Plus, she only said a minute.*

"You can just step outside of the door. I will call you back in as soon as we're finished talking."

"All right," my mom said as she opened the door. She looked back at me and smiled as she walked through and closed the door behind her. The doctor waited a few more seconds, then pulled out a stool from behind the other side of the exam bed, which I hadn't seen before and rolled it over to about two feet in front of me. She sat down and looked at me.

"The reason why I asked your mom to leave the room for a minute is so I could ask you some questions and you can feel free to tell me the truth, without having to worry about what your mother thinks or knows, ok?" I nodded my head in agreement. *Oh wow,* I thought, *this is very thoughtful,* still curious as to what she wanted to know that I wouldn't want to tell my mother. *Could she possibly know that I snuck down into the kitchen the other night and cut myself a slice of cheesecake? That I sometimes cursed on the bus on the way to school? What could it be?*

"Janelle, I am going to ask you some questions and you can feel perfectly safe with me. It goes no further than me and you and this room, I won't tell anyone else, is that ok?" Again, I nodded my head in anticipation.

"Janelle have you ever had sex?" she asked calmly with a warm expression on her face. *Oh!* I thought, my eyes widening in shock. *I wasn't expecting her to ask that!*

"No!" I said emphatically. I was definitely shocked.

"It's ok if you are sexually active, I just need to know so I can better be able to help you."

"No, I am not." I said again, now with more of a sense of urgency. I needed her to understand that I had not had sex. I had to talk about sex with my mother when I was 5 years old in kindergarten when the teachers sent home a letter to all the parents letting them know that one of the students came into class telling all the other students where babies "really came from." And they didn't come from storks! That was also the same student who told us earlier that year that Santa wasn't real. I learned a lot of life lessons in kindergarten, what can I say?! That sex talk with my mom wasn't the most comfortable, but I remember my mother saying that I shouldn't have it until I was married, because it was something that only married couples do. I was just starting to think that boys are cute, well a certain boy in my class, maybe, not all boys. And we were *nowhere* near having sex. I was lucky if he even touched my hand by accident while completing a project in school!

I looked her straight in the eye and repeated, "No, I am not."

"Ok, well that's good to know. Now we can let your mother back in." I felt a wave of relief. Like I passed some type of test. She opened the door and motioned for my mother to come back in.

"Ok, well, tell me a little more about your menstrual cycle history. When was the last time you had your period?"

"Two weeks ago," my mother responded. I was happy to have her respond for me again.

"Ok, got it. All right, well let's go ahead and have a look, shall we?.

After a quick pelvic exam, the doctor slid a stool between myself and my mother. "Well," she began, "I know why we're having problems inserting the tampon."

Well that's a relief.

"You see," she began, "Young girls typically have a hymen. A small thin layer of membranous tissue that is just behind the vaginal opening." My mother and I nodded our heads in unison. "For most girls it's thin with a small hole in the middle of it. But large enough for a tampon to be inserted through." Again, my mom and I nodded. "Some girls who exercise very vigorously or ride horses will have the hymen break on its own and it goes away."

Yes, I vaguely remember hearing about that.

"So getting back to the size of the hole. Some girls have a singular small hole. For others it's big. And then there is the smallest number of girls who have two small holes." Again, we nodded. "Well, Janelle is one of those girls who has two small holes. Both of which are so small it will not let a tampon through." We nodded and I raised my eyebrows in curiosity at this new news. "And not only are there two tiny holes in her hymen, it is also the thickest hymen I have ever encountered in my life." And there it was... the other shoe slamming to the ground. "That is why it hurt when you tried to insert the tampon and it wouldn't go through." She ended.

The thickest hymen she had ever encountered?!?! I am a freak of nature! Two holes and thickest hymen. This can't be good. My mind started spiraling.

"So, is there anything we can do?" My mother asked calmly.

Great question mom!

"Well, I could break the hymen for you," the doctor said while looking down at me. "It would be painful for a day and you would have some vaginal bleeding after. But then after that you should be ok and will definitely be able to use a tampon." I imagine at this point, my face may have looked something like a deer caught in headlights.

Break it? And it will hurt... of course it will hurt. It hurt trying to put the tampon in. I don't want that kind of pain. And the bleeding after. I don't want that either. How on earth would she even break the "thickest hymen in the world"? Is there another option? Again, my mind was reeling.

My mother looked down at me and I am going to guess, registered the panic that was escaping from my mind and going directly to my face because after a pause she asked, "And that's the only option?"

"At this point," the doctor responded while sighing. "If we don't break it now, we can wait and see if it gets thinner over time. And of course, we don't have to do it now. You can always think about it or come back another time, if you change your mind." Again, my mom and I nodded our heads.

"Ok, well, Janelle, do you want to have the doctor break it for you?" She looked down at me calmly.

Uhm that would be an absolute NO. But instead, I said quietly, "no."

My mom nodded once and looked back at the doctor, "Ok, so we will not be doing that today. But if we change our mind then we will make another appointment and come back."

"Ok, sounds good to me." She stuck out her hand to me. "Well, Janelle, it was nice to meet you. I hope the next time I see you, you can tell me about all of the races you have won." I took her hand and shook it, smiling up at her. *Apart from wanting to hurt me in the most private of places, she's not that bad.*

She then shook my mom's hand, "It's good to see you again, Mrs. Villiers."

"Likewise." My mom returned the handshake. Then the doctor opened the door and directed us back to the waiting room.

"Just stop by the front desk on your way out. And have a great day ladies!" The doctor said as we made our way down the hall.

We both waved back at the doctor and headed to the waiting room. My mom paid the co-pay, we left the office and got into our car to drive home. I was lost in my thoughts...

I have the thickest hymen in the world...I'm some sort of freak!

This did not help to create a self-image of myself as a beautiful, intelligent, desired young woman. Now, I'm thinking: *my poor future-husband, when he tries to have sex with me, he won't be able to get his penis through my hymen AND it's going to be really painful.* No one ever imagines their first time is going to be painful or at least they hope it won't be. I, on the other hand, now knew, without any doubt, it would. More thoughts reaffirming my shame-based ways of looking at myself crept into my mind: *What guy would want to be with a freak of nature like me? I'm not pretty. I am definitely not desirable. I am not loveable.*

Chapter 4: "We should not judge people by their peak of excellence; but by the distance they have traveled from the point where they started." – Henry Ward Beecher

This is a public announcement: The next 3 chapters not only give more context for why I felt a lot of shame around sex and my sexuality but they also serve a point of validation for all the woman, (you, a friend or family member), who have ever had pain during sex that they could not explain.

You Are Not Alone.

While I was in undergrad I lost my virginity to one of the first men I ever loved. He was a year older than me, super intelligent, but couldn't let anyone in his high school (HS) know that he was, because at the time, it was "not cool." It's not like now where "nerds" or "smart kids" in HS are believed to become extremely successful in a lucrative tech company, or founding one, in the future. So, instead of going to college, he enlisted in the military to pay for his education. He was cute, kind, affectionate, loved having fun and trying new things and he just seemed to "get me." He was the first boyfriend I ever had whom I felt so comfortable to be myself with, that I actually let my "always be perfect" guard down and argued with him. All the other boyfriends before him never saw the real me because I was too busy trying to make them like me.

Why was I like that? Why was I so scared to be myself? Why did I always want to please? One reason, I now know, is because I was living from a shame-based belief. Oftentimes, those of us who are shame-based in our thinking, will live their lives with a mask on. We believe, as I did at the time, that if any guy got to know the *real* me he wouldn't like me, because the real me is unlovable and I was trying to spare myself the hurt of being abandoned if he saw the real me. Additionally, I am now aware of the instinctive ways that men and women act around each other, thanks to the relationship expert Alison Armstrong. She describes that women have prehistoric urges, drives and/or instincts that affect us in modern society. For example, the desire to be protected from dangerous animals, like tigers. I think, looking back, that I had a strong instinctive urge to please the guy to make sure the guy would stick around to protect me. I was scared that if I didn't please him, or if he was disappointed by me, that he would abandon me, that he wouldn't stick around to protect me (from the tiger), either. This fear is so strong I could never really be myself. Do you ever remember being like that in a relationship, kind reader? Do you remember ever having this feeling? It's so compulsive and yet the exact opposite of what we want to do if we want to have a strong long-lasting relationship. Or maybe it's just me...

To my complete surprise and joy, this boyfriend made me feel like he liked me for who I really was, even if I disagreed with him. And so, I was shocked the first time we had an argument! I couldn't even tell you what it was about. I just remember we were on the phone and I had this feeling that I strongly disagreed with him... or that what he just said was supremely "wrong" and I definitely had the "right" answer. And we went back and forth for a while. I remember getting very passionate about being right and then catching myself.

"Wow! I think that was the first time I have ever argued with a boyfriend..."

"Really? That's interesting. Why have you never had an argument before?"

"I don't think I cared enough about the others to want to really get my opinion out, even if... or especially if, it doesn't agree with what they are thinking or saying."

"Really? Does that mean that you really care about me then?" He teased.

"Yea... it does!" I teased back. "I mean I never felt comfortable enough, in other relationships, to be myself, to say my real opinion without having a fear that the argument would cause us to break up. It's like I had this thought in my head that good couples don't argue. And couples that argue, break up." A thought many people have when they haven't learned about crucial conversations and how to have them. A good book that helped me (fifteen years later) understand these conversations and how to engage in them is "Crucial Conversations: Tools for Talking When Stakes Are High" by Kerry Patterson, Joseph Grenny , Ron McMillan and Al Switzler.

"I see... Where did you get that idea from? That doesn't really make much sense."

"I know... saying it out loud just now, it doesn't make any sense at all! But that's what I was thinking and feeling about arguments."

"Well, I'm glad you don't feel that way with me. I want you to be yourself. That's who I fell in love with." I started to blush.

And I really liked and then loved him for who he was and I wanted to physically show him that. I am grateful for that and for him, for not taking my decision to lose my virginity to him lightly. I decided to tear my hymen for him... remember I had the "thickest hymen my mom's gynecologist had ever seen"...

Side bar: it hurt... a LOT!

As the glorious months of having a boyfriend I loved whom I actually made love to marched on, so did his responsibilities in the military. Things got harder. We were already long distance and he had to move to a base even further away than where he was currently located. His schedule and mine became busier and we had fewer times when we could talk. And I missed him like crazy but started to fear that he didn't miss me as much as I missed him. But my shame-based thinking kicked in again and I thought: *I've been living in a fantasy! There is no way he could really love "unlovable" me. It's much more likely that he would start to fall in love with a prettier, more attractive girl on his base. Someone whom he could see more regularly than me.* So, I decided to break up with him before he could break up with me, before he could hurt me. *Always, one step ahead of the game*, I thought. I know, it's super cliche but there's no point in lying about it now.

With my next boyfriend I wanted to be smart. I knew condoms weren't always reliable so I started taking birth control pills. Because there was no way on this earth that I was going to get pregnant while I was in college. And my institution was giving out birth control pills like they were candy. Because they *also* didn't want anyone to get pregnant. The message they sent to us girls on campus was clear: You are obviously having sex, so take these pills so you won't get pregnant. Because at Ivy League schools, we can't have girls getting knocked up. Concentrate on your career first, then worry about kids later. So, I did what all the responsible, sexually active college students in a committed relationship would do. I got birth control pills and used them exactly as prescribed. Then I started to lose interest in my new boyfriend. He was a boy from my town whom I had a crush on when I was fourteen years old. He had made a decision to discontinue attending his college in New York and worked at a big-name athletic shoe and clothing store. He had no internal ambition to become a manager, or to own his own business. Quite frankly, his life was the same every day with no sign of him wanting to do better or be better, it seemed like I was always pushing him to try new things. He had no internal gumption. Around that same time, I also noticed that I was starting to have pain when we had sex. *Maybe it's the type of condom?* We changed that and it still hurt. *Maybe I have an infection?* I went to the campus women's health center and had a lovely conversation with my nurse practitioner.

"Well, the reason you are feeling pain is because you have a yeast infection. But don't worry, these are common. Take these pills and after you are finished and the infection has cleared you can go back to your regular sexual activity and you shouldn't have any pain."

Well, I did as she said and it worked! I was so relieved. And then the pain came back. But this time, I knew what to do! So, I went back to the women's health center. After an examination the nurse looked at me and said, "Well, there is no sign of any yeast, but I'm sure that must be what's causing the pain. I'll give you another dose of Diflucan and that should do the trick."

"Thank you so much!" I walked out feeling confident with the Diflucan, knowing that in a few days I would be better. But a week later... I wasn't. There was still a lot of pain upon penetration. I told my boyfriend, "This hurts. I can't do this."

"I understand, no problem, let's just cuddle and watch a movie." This was music to my ears, the first time. But the next time we tried and it hurt, I was annoyed and frustrated. What was worse was that all the things that I thought were cute about him were now annoying. If we were out in public, or around my friends who I feared could now see the annoying traits that I saw, I was embarrassed by him. Embarrassed that they would ask each other behind my back: how could Janelle be with a guy who isn't going anywhere in life? And I started not to be interested in having sex with him. And when we did have sex, it hurt. I would go back to the women's health center over and over and sometimes they saw yeast and sometimes they didn't and no matter if it was seen or not, each time I was given Diflucan.

Eventually, I couldn't take it anymore and I tried to think of ways to be mean to him so he would break up with me. I started fights, was overly dramatic when he annoyed me. But it didn't work fast enough. He didn't seem to want to break up with me, even when I was being my worst self. So, eventually I had to tell him I wanted to end it. I found a stupid and petty, reason for I wanted to break up and he didn't believe me. He didn't think it was a "good enough reason to break up." He didn't take me saying that I wanted to break up seriously at all. So, instead of a civilized break up, it turned into a messy one. You see, kind reader, I was given advice by a good friend: "Sometimes the breakup needs to be messy and mean so that way both sides know it's over for good." So, that's exactly what I did, I was mean and cruel. I remember yelling at him while we were outside an engineering building on campus. I don't recall what I was saying as I was yelling. I just remember yelling at the top of my lungs. One thing I *do* remember is that I eventually said "I don't want to be with you anymore, get away from me!" He was trying to get me to lower my voice and come closer to me, thinking that the closer he got I wouldn't need to yell. But I was committed to being my worst self. I screamed again, "Get away from me," while lunging at him with my hands to push him back. He caught my hands to try to prevent me from pushing him which resulted in me trying to move my hands even faster to push him and in the scuffle, I ended up mushing him in his face. Because my nails were long at that time, they scratched him across his cheek leaving a small red line of a welt. I stopped in mid horror. I hate violence and it is not my usual mode of operation. I couldn't believe I had just done that. "Did you just scratch me across my face?!" he asked in shock. *Oh God! Is he bleeding?!* I thought in a panic. But I quickly recovered. *I have to keep up with the crazy so he will finally leave me alone*, I thought. "Just get out of here!" I yelled at him. He held up his hand to his cheek, which I thought had started bleeding a little. He looked at me as if he didn't recognize me and finally walked away. I was definitely the "bitch" in this breakup and although I was embarrassed to play that role, I was also relieved. It worked! And I was finally free of him. Free to disconnect from someone who was going nowhere in life. Free to look at possibilities of other directions my life could go that would never include him. Free to find a better protector and a potential provider. These truths were the ones I know would hurt him even more than my accidental slap in the face. Confronting him with the truth seemed like too harsh of a thing to do. It seemed to me that creating a "mean girl" character was much easier. But would it have been? What if I had told him the truth? Would it have changed anything? I'm not convinced that it would have. He may have promised to change but that may have only delayed our inevitable breakup. I will never know. However, a particular pattern was definitely emerging. My willingness to do anything to avoid emotional confrontation. In this case I literally chose physical confrontation over emotional confrontation.

Newly single, I wondered if my "pain-with-sex" problems would go away. With the first partner after the breakup, it didn't hurt the first time, but it definitely hurt the second time. And I was even less invested in that relationship. He went to a different university in Philly and had completely different interests than my own. The only thing that was interesting about him is that he was interested in me. He thought I was attractive and paid for food and I was still a broke college student. So, that relationship ended quickly. And of course, at the Women's Health Center I was given more Diflucan. Maybe there was yeast, maybe there wasn't. Either way I took the medicine and knew that I wasn't having sex for a while so no matter what, I would heal and then move on with my life.

And that I did, I graduated from my very difficult undergraduate program. *Thank you, God!* I was supposed to land some amazing job paying a huge salary. Fast forward, that didn't happen. I ended up working in a laboratory, making only $30,000 a year, living in NYC? Yes, I know I'll wait for you to stop laughing before we continue, but please know I honestly thought that was a lot! I was definitely young and naive. Ultimately, I was convinced that I didn't learn anything about how to live as an adult that I should have learned while in school. Like how much your salary should be if you want to live in a decent apartment in NYC. But I blundered around, met some guys and had one more sexual partner and guess what... It still hurt. And that ever present shame-based thinking started to become louder in my head: *What's wrong with you? You are still a freak. You can't even have sex without pain. You are undesirable and definitely unlovable.*

Talking with my friends was like talking to a character from *Sex and The City*. Everyone was enjoying sex and having a good time. Feelings may have been messy, but the act of sex seemed to be enjoyable and fun for everyone. And if you think I didn't have a case of Fear-of-Missing-Out (FOMO) you are *wrong*. Not only did I yearn to have the sexual, freeing, escapades my friends and the characters of my favorite show at the time, *Sex and The City*, were having, I was also convinced that eventually my sex problems would just go away. Then I met the man who would become my first husband. And I'm not sure if it was because it had been so long since I had had sex, but I finally was exclusively with someone and when we had sex it did not hurt. I was thrilled and relieved and enjoyed it! *Maybe I'm not a freak after all. Maybe I am desirable and loveable.*

I remember when we first met. I was introduced to him by his room-mate. The two of them lived across the hall from me in a multi-family home. He didn't stand out to me and I wasn't that attracted to him, to be honest. He was three years younger than me (a teenager) and into the latest gadgets and fashion. That was not me!

Until one day, he was able to answer a riddle in a book that required, in my opinion, a certain level of intelligence, a level that I found extremely attractive. Apparently, my being older than him didn't bother him.

And so, we started to date...

You know how the honeymoon phase goes, right? Everything was great!

For our first date we went to a glow in the dark mini-golf course. I remember laughing a lot. We had a lot of fun.

I remember during that first year of our dating that I got flowers for Valentine's Day, while I was preparing our Valentine's Day dinner. I don't even like flowers, but I was thankful for the thought. After I was given the flowers, he left my apartment to go lie down because he had a "bad day." He then refused to talk to me for the rest of the night. And my shame-based thinking kicked into gear: *You are not good enough, you have no value, you're a freak. What man would want to be with you? Not even this man wants you to be around him.* You know the Maya Angelou quote "People don't remember what you did. They don't remember what you said. But they remember how you made them feel." Well, the combination of what he did and my shame-based thinking led me to feel that he didn't want to be around me, like my existence bothered him, and that the flowers he had given were a performative act of him doing his Valentine's Day duty. It was the first time he made me feel of little value in our relationship.

Then there was the first time we got into an argument...

One random night, I took a nap to be well-rested and awake for him when he returned home. While I was asleep, he called multiple times, but I didn't hear the phone ring or feel it vibrating while I was sleeping. I finally woke up to see multiple missed calls and got worried that some-thing had happened to him. I immediately called him back, filled with concern as the phone rang and I waited for him to answer. And when he finally did, I was met with an alarmingly aggressive response and a barrage of questions about what I was doing and *with whom* I was doing it with?

I remember being so upset because I took a nap to be well rested for *him*. And the reward for this was being yelled at and accused of the craziest thing! I was being accused of being with another man, when all I wanted to do was be at my best for *him*! It was infuriating! In the middle of all his yelling I finally yelled back "I can't believe you really think that I am here with some other dude when I am here getting rest for *you.*" This was met by more yelling on his end related to who I was with this whole time and he didn't believe I was sleeping. Then I just said "you know what Fuck You!" And hung up the phone.

I know! Not my best moment. And there was probably a way better way of handling that situation... but I remember thinking: *who is he to yell at me the way he did and accusing me! I don't need this kind of stress. Not even my parents yell at me the way he did when I don't pick up the phone when they call.*

He called back soon after and then instantly started telling me how disrespectful and horrible I was for saying "Fuck you" to him. I immediately apologized, but it was too late! I was the horrible person and he was the victim, and now he was mad at me and hung up on me. Of course, I try to call back to apologize, but now he was not picking up my calls. My first thought was to reach out to his best friend. So I called his best friend and told him what happened. He agreed it wasn't the best way to respond, but that he also understood why I was so upset. He advised me to let him calm down and talk to him when he got home. I took his advice.

I remember we talked. I remember feeling like somehow the tables were flipped from me doing absolutely nothing wrong, to him now having a reason to be mad at me because "how could I 'disrespect him' and say 'fuck you' to him like that?"

I remember not wanting to sleep next to him that night because I was so angry and going into the living room to do push-ups to release some steam.

That was the first time the tables were turned on me... I naively thought it would be the last.

They say hindsight is 20/20. For me, that is an understatement. That entire first argument was a huge red flag that is so clear to me now, but wasn't clear then. My shame-based thinking was fearful that he thought this sign of my disrespect towards him was also an indication of my unworthiness, my unlovableness, and I didn't want him to leave me because of that. This, in combination with the instinctual fear of "losing my protector". I definitely didn't want to lose that either. But these instincts and shame-based feelings were colliding with other healthier thoughts that I managed to build up to this point, such that: I did have value and I shouldn't be treated that way. But, ultimately the instinct won over, and I felt the need to bend and keep apologizing in order to make sure he stayed with me.

Someone once told me that narcissistic people or those with narcissistic tendencies need someone to call them out on their crap. And that may have been me in the beginning. But if the narcissist sees any inadequacy, they will manipulate that to their advantage and use it against you to make you always feel small. They will make it seem that you are in the wrong, making themselves the victim. Sadly, I confess that it didn't take long for this "huge" inadequacy to come up. Because not too long after that argument, I started having pain with sex. And *who could ever love a woman who was always in pain when you tried to have sex with her? When you tried to connect with her? Her one primal job is to please her man sexually. And she can't even do that!*

It started off as a little pain and I could get through having sex with him, but then it was too much, and I had to stop. I only knew to say one thing, "I must have a yeast infection. I will make an appointment with the doctor. But we won't be able to have sex for at least seven days after, when I am cured from the yeast infection."

"What?! Seven days?! That's such a long time!" He responded in shock.

"I know, I know. But it will be over before you know it and the infection will be gone and it won't hurt. Otherwise, if we do something in between the seven days then it may not go away and I will have pain again," I attempted to explain.

"Ok, ok. I understand," but nothing about his demeanor looked like he understood or wanted to understand. It was like I was punishing him and he was just "taking it."

I'm such a freak. I can't believe he's still here with me. I'm not loveable.

Chapter 5:
Vulvadynia – I'm
sorry, Vulva... what?

I went to my current, very friendly GYN and sure enough she found yeast and I was given Diflucan. I dutifully took the medication right away and waited the seven days, and even eight for good measure. And, well, our next time I thought *that didn't hurt as bad. So, maybe it will get better and I will feel less pain.* But it did not. I went through episodes where I would take the pain until I couldn't take it anymore and then would go back to the GYN. Most times there was, in fact, yeast present, but enough times when there was not. On one visit that was only two weeks after the last visit, I remember sitting at the edge of the exam table waiting for her to come in.

She knocked on the exam room door I was in.

"Come in," I said. She was a Jewish woman in her late 50's early 60's. A little plump, with short curly brown hair that softly framed her face. She was on the shorter side of life, much like me, because when we stood in front of each other we were eye-to-eye and I'm only 5'3"...the short side of life. My doctor walked into the room while looking down at my chart in her hands. Presumably she was looking at the sheet I filled out in the waiting room which asked: "What is your reason for coming in today" My answer on the sheet of paper: "I have a yeast infection."

"Hello Janelle," she said warmly and finally looked up from the chart and straight at me. "So, I see that you were just here with us a little over two weeks ago!" She raised her eyebrows up at me in what seemed like mock surprise.

"Yes. Yes, that is true." I responded.

"Ah I see." And without skipping a beat, "You're quite a frequent flier here with us, aren't ya?!" and she cracked a smile. I couldn't help but chuckle. *"Frequent flier to the GYN office"* That is correct. That is exactly what I had become.

"Yes," I was still chuckling, "Yes, I guess I am."

"So, what brings you into us today?" She looked back down at the chart. "You think you have another yeast infection?"

"Yes, I'm pretty sure that I do."

"And why is that?"

"I'm having pain with sex again. It's usually my first sign."

"Ah, I see. Well, the last time you came in, I didn't see any yeast. I remember I gave you Diflucan and we sent off labs to see if it was a special type of yeast that doesn't respond to Diflucan. Let me check those results and then we will do a physical exam."

"Ok, sounds good," I replied. She rolled her chair in front of the computer in the room and began looking up results.

"Well, I have your results here. The good news is they didn't find any of that unusual yeast I was telling you about. The other news is, is that it doesn't look like there was any yeast at all, that last time you were here. Based on the symptoms you are describing to me, I think I may know what's going on here. But let's first do the physical exam and see if we see anything else."

I nodded my head in agreement.

During the exam she placed her finger on the opening of my vagina and it definitely hurt. "Ow!"

"Ok so where I just touched is definitely inflamed and irritated."

A few minutes later the exam was done.

"Well," she began. "It's just as I thought, there is absolutely no sign of yeast. But you are definitely irritated and inflamed along the vaginal opening. Janelle, I believe it's possible that you have a condition that's causing this. I want you to know, first of all, that this pain that you are feeling is *not...in...your...head.*" She said this last part slowly with conviction. Almost as if she were my lawyer defending my case to a judge. I nodded my head in agreement and in relief to know it wasn't in my head. I never thought it was, but it became very clear in that instant that some women may experience the pain I feel and it could be psycho-somatic. For example, it could be emotional trauma causing them to feel pain. Otherwise known as "all in their head." But it was clear that my doctor wanted me to know that I was not in that group. And from her demeanor I could also tell that she needed me to know this so that I would and could defend myself to others. It was a fleeting thought but I distinctly remember thinking *Ok, this is not in my head. The doctor is absolutely certain it's not in my head. Remember that, Janelle, so you can tell others when they ask.* She went on, "I have seen cases like this before, where women are told it's all in their head when they have pain but no infection. I want you to know that that is not you. You definitely have tissue that is inflamed, irritated and causing you pain. I have also heard that a small dose of antidepressant medication may help with this. So, I am going to prescribe for you a dose that is one quarter of the typical dose necessary for depression but has been known to help with the chronic inflammation that you are experiencing around your vaginal opening. It's supposed to help with overactive nerve endings." I nodded as if I understood. But admittedly, in that moment, I had no idea what anti-depressant medication had anything to do with my vagina and my ability to have sex without pain. That bewilderment must have come across my face, because she added, "You are not depressed. Do you understand? I am not saying that you are depressed. However, this medication has been found to have an alternate affect when given in very small doses, for women who have had what you are currently experiencing."

"Oooh ok." I nodded again. This time her explanation seemed clearer.

A few minutes later I left the office a new prescription in my hand for what the character on *Sex & The City*, Charlotte, said of her once similar diagnosis, "a depressed vagina." But I was hopeful. Seven days later after dutifully taking my lite antidepressant we tried again.

And H A L L E L U J A H... absolutely NO pain! Not even the little that I would suffer through just to please my then boyfriend. It was absolutely euphoric! We were both so happy! And then... a week later, it was back. Just a little pain, the little pain I would have mustered through normally. But now that I had experienced what sex was supposed to feel like, I knew immediately that this was not ok. A few days later I was back at my GYN's office.

While sitting in a chair in the exam room, my GYN sat across from me in her own chair.

"Well it worked!" I began to tell her, "until a week later and it stopped working. I feel the pain again."

"Oh, I'm so sorry, my dear. I was hoping that this would really be able to help you."

"I know! Me too!" I looked down a little glumly.

"Well," she continued, "I could up the dose somewhat, but I don't believe that's going to really help. I think now it's time to call in a professional who knows more about this than I do."

"Oh, ok."

"Yes, I have a list here of a few doctors who are considered experts in the field and can help you. There are very few of them, I must warn you. However, I am sure at least one of them must be here in New York City."

I nodded in hopefulness as she began to look in the computer for her list of experts.

"Ok, this one is in Chicago, this one is in California, this one is in New York but it seems like only for a few days out of the year, he is mainly in Washington DC, so that won't really work. But maybe you could go to DC..." she trailed off as she continued to scroll down her small list, and then... "Ok here we go, Dr. Smith! He practices here in New York City, Midtown West." She started to write down his name, number and address for me on a piece of paper.

"Here you go! I would recommend you contact him as soon as you can, so we can get you the help you deserve. Remember, this is **not** in your head!" She handed me the paper.

"Thank you so much!" I was so relieved to be given the name and contact info of an expert. There was hope on the horizon...

Maybe I am not a freak after all. Maybe someone can help fix me.

A few months after this appointment, because my boyfriend's immigration status was about to be very uncertain we decided to elope. We figured that would eliminate one of our biggest stressors at the time, his ability to stay in the country. A few weeks after we eloped, I met with Dr. Smith in his small Midtown West High-rise office. Which turned out to be his apartment. Of course, he was a specialist who was not considered "in-network" for my insurance and so now my husband and I had to come up with $800 to see him. That may not seem like a lot to you. However, for two young people, neither making over $45,000 a year while living in New York City, this was a whole lot!

To be honest, the office seemed a bit sketchy... creepy even. I was unaccompanied, and I was definitely alone with a man in what was supposed to be his office but was definitely his apartment. The "office" was complete with a couch, loveseat and lounge chair that was next to some sort of monitor that looked medical in nature as it had a lot of wires coming out of it.

He welcomed me in, warmly enough. I sat on the love seat while he sat across from me on the couch as I recounted my tale of vaginal pain and woe.

"Well," he began after my story finished, "this definitely sounds like a case of vulvodynia caused by your pelvic floor muscles being too weak. I believe this is the classic case where we will have to strengthen your muscles."

After a very creepy exam in his office. He prescribed a muscle training program that required a $1,200 device to keep track of my progress.

"Ok great. So just contact me as soon as you're ready to purchase it and we can get you started with a training program." He smiled down at me. The appointment ended and I left the creepy apartment/office in Midtown West feeling utterly dejected and like a failure. My shame-based thinking kicked in, *I am the freak with a weak pelvic floor, the freak who can't have sex with her husband. Who could love a woman like this? And the only way I can get back to normal is to come up with money I do not have. The job I have is obviously not a successful one if I can't afford this treatment. I'm a failure AND I'm a freak.*

What was I going to do?

"So, mom and dad, I have something I need to talk to you about..." The conversation was just as humiliating and awkward as I anticipated it would be. However, my parents, God bless them, took it in stride and were the epitome of support. They were able to give us half the money and suggested I reach out to other family members who were in medicine or who worked in health care who may be able to get the same device at a discounted price. However, I had exhausted the amount of mortification I was willing to put myself through and decided we would figure out how to get the rest of the money on our own. And, eventually, months later, we did.

The prescription was simple. All I had to do was squeeze and hold exercises for 10 minutes twice per day (morning and night) at least 4-5 times per week and no sex for a month while doing the muscle therapy.

The last bit of instruction brought on feelings of pure dread. Telling my husband that we weren't going to be able to have sex for about a month (maybe even two) was going to be another difficult conversation. I was sure he would look at me with despondency and revulsion. A look I was getting from him pretty regularly now. I was correct. After I told him that we were instructed not to have sex for a month and maybe two, while I started my treatment, the look I got was, indeed, a mix of being letdown and loathing, just as I thought it would be. I left that conversation, like I had the previous ones feeling less than dirt. This turned up the volume on my now frequent (almost constant) shame-based thoughts: *I deserve these looks of loathing. I am unworthy of love. I am a freak of nature. I am unworthy.*

So, at home, I practiced and exercised, admittedly not as exact as prescribed. There were days where I would only have time to do it in the morning and not at night and other days where I missed exercising all together because of my demanding graduate school schedule. I was not used to making my health a priority. *I mean why would someone who thinks that she has no value put her own health as a priority?*

But if I am really honest, no one prepared me for how humiliating it would be to use the device at home, many times in front of my husband. Each time I took the device out of the drawer to use it, I swear he would give me a look that was a mix of discomfort, disgust, and disappointment. The energy in the room immediately shifted to a heightened awkwardness. And I couldn't blame him. I felt those feelings about myself. It was like my body was rebelling against me and wouldn't allow me to perform the one basic act that all women are to be able to do for their husbands: Have (pain free) sex. I felt disconnected, isolated and alone - SHAME. Brene Brown defines shame as the intensely painful feeling or experience of believing we are flawed and therefore unworthy of acceptance and belonging. Shame creates feelings of fear, blame and disconnection. That was me, feeling fear (of losing my husband and protector), blaming myself for being a freak and completely disconnected from him or any other woman regarding this topic. The doctors made comments like there are other women who had gone through what I was going through. However, none of those women were in my life. And there was no one I could share my deepest sorrows, fears, concerns and disappointments with, except God. This routine went on for about four to six months. And to our dismay and further disappointment it did not help. I did not get better nor improve. The shame that I felt was compounded by how my husband treated me, which derived from feelings that alternated between disgust and anger. Infidelity soon followed, which added another layer to my shame.

And I don't mean he was cheating on me with one woman. It was with multiple women for almost the remainder of our marriage. I didn't find out about all of these until after we split up. But there was one time that I knew for sure.

On the morning of a very big exam, I had for grad school, I noticed a notification pop up on his phone. I knew I shouldn't look at his phone; something told me not to look. But I looked anyway. And to my horror, the message that came through said: "Carla: So, are we going to fuck again at lunch today?" I showed him the message.

"What's this?!" I asked him as I shoved his phone with the message in his face. "Is this what's going to happen at lunch today?!"

"So, is this it? Are we going to end things now?" He responded calmly. Too calmly. He wasn't even trying to come up with a story for the message. It was like he was resigned. Maybe even slightly relieved. My mind was spinning. *Who was this girl? Did they really have sex yesterday at lunch? I'm so stupid for thinking my husband would be faithful to me. She must think I'm an idiot. Maybe I deserve this. I can't give him sex the way he wants. Oh my God I have an exam I have to go to! I have to focus!*

"I can't answer that right now. I have a really important exam I have to go take right now." I threw the phone on the bed and walked out. An hour later, fighting back tears, I took my exam and would love to tell you I passed it. But I didn't... I failed it.

Brene Brown has noted in her shame research that a particular aspect of shame that comes up is that we feel that the disconnect we are experiencing while in shame is *deserved*. I can certainly identify with that feeling during this time in my life. I felt alone, disconnected, undesirable and also like I didn't *deserve* connection or to be loved because I was a freak, a completely unlovable person who didn't deserve anything other than to be cheated on and left to live a life of sadness and isolation. *I should have known. How could I have ever thought that I was enough. I have been a freak and unworthy to be loved since the day I was born.*

On the other side of all of this is that we had no idea that what I was being trained to do was in fact the exact *opposite* of what I eventually needed to do to heal, restore and improve my situation.

Perhaps a year or more later, while in graduate school, while I attended my annual GYN appointment at the Student Health Center on campus, I finally got my next breakthrough. I had been to the Student Health Center a number of times, becoming a "frequent flier" there, as well, for my frequent "yeast infections". This time, coming in for my annual, the nurse asked a lot more questions than with my other visits. These questions allowed me to open up about my sexual past and current situation. The nurse listened to me with empathy and when I finished my description of symptoms she finally asked, "So, with this last doctor you went to, it didn't help?"

"No unfortunately, not. Even with all the money we spent on the medical device and equipment." I bent my head down and stared at my hands. I was emotionally drained just by talking about all of this.

"You know, just the other night, there was a doctor and his patients who were being interviewed on the show "60 minutes." These women described having symptoms like yours and the years that it took them to find a diagnosis until they found this doctor. What was his name..." she trailed off and looked to the right trying to recall the doctor's name whom she had seen. "I think it was something that began with a G, if I'm not mistaken. But I can't remember it exactly. But I am sure if we found him and put you in touch with him, he could surely help!"

I perked up. *What?! There were other women talking about my condition on TV and there was a doctor who helped them?! Is this for real?*

"Yes, I'm quite certain. You know what. Let's do a Google search, I am sure we can find something." She swiveled her chair to face her computer, found the Google search engine and began typing in the search box. Not being able to contain my excitement, I hopped up from my chair and stood behind her looking over her shoulder to peer at the computer screen with her.

"Let's see... 'Pain with sex doctor'..." she typed in the search but nothing came up that looked like the right thing.

"Or... 'Doctor on 60 minutes'..." she typed in next. But way too many doctors populated the search results.

"Or what about... '60 minutes show Doctor Vagina'..." after she typed that in the search and pressed enter on the keyboard the results populated and at the very top was a link to the show 60 minutes and Vulvadynia. "This must be it!" she said enthusiastically. "It was just posted this past Sunday."

"Oh great!" I was trying to hold back the welling excitement that was bubbling up inside, as she clicked on the link. The page opened and it described an interview with Dr. Andrew Goldstein and his patients with Vulvadynia.

"That's him!" She exclaimed. "Dr. Goldstein! I knew it started with a G! Dr. Andrew Goldstein, that's him!"

"Oh wonderful!" *I can't believe she found him!*

"Let's look up his office," she said as she typed in his full name and title in the Google search. The results were full of links about Dr. Goldstein and his expertise with Vulvodynia. She found a link that was associated with his direct office. "Here we go..." she trailed off as she scrolled down through his website to find a phone number and address. "Here it is... 'to make an appointment please call the office,'" she read from the website. "And here are the addresses. Oh! He has an office in D.C. *and* in New York City. Wonderful!" She grabbed a pen and paper and began writing his name, phone number and the two addresses down for me. I couldn't believe it! The first sign of real hope in a very long time! She finished writing with a flourish and spun around and handed me the paper.

"Well, Janelle," she said as she beamed up at me, "based on what I saw yesterday, this is definitely the doctor who can help you, as he, apparently, helped so many others. I would say give his office a call today!"

"Thank you *so* much!" I gushed as I took the paper from her outstretched hand. I was blinking back tears of joy and dare I say it... relief.

"Oh, it's nothing at all! I'm just so glad I happened to see that interview on TV the other night."

"Me too!"

"Well, Janelle... Good luck! You can email me later and let me know how it goes!" She turned back to her desk, picked up her business card and handed it to me. "My email is on this."

"Thank you so much!" I hurried out of the office, paper and business card in hand. As soon as I found a quiet place, I took out my cell phone and dialed the number on the piece of paper. A friendly voice picked up after three rings.

"Dr. Goldstein's office. How may I help you?"

Chapter 6: Finally Finding Dr. G!

It was a six month wait to get an appointment in his New York City office. But the next opening in the D.C. office was as early as three weeks from today. I took it! His friendly receptionist emailed me all of the forms that needed to be filled out before my arrival. The forms included the fact that he did not take insurance and the fee to see him was in the hundreds of dollars and depending on the treatment after evaluation, could be about $1,000. Fortunately, at this point my husband's health insurance came with a flexible spending account (FSA), where he had already opted for the maximum amount possible to be placed in the account. Those funds could then be accessed by using a special pre-paid Visa card that I could use at Dr. G's office. We dotted all "I's" and crossed our "T's" and made sure we could make the appointment happen. The only concern now was getting to DC and then once in DC how do I get to his office? The year was 2008 and Uber was not in DC (or NYC) until 2011. Also, my husband could not drive me, nor go with me because it was during a week-day and he had to be at work. So, I contacted my college roommate who happened to be in D.C. at the time studying for her Ph.D. in psychology. It was so good to catch up with her and tell her what was going on.

"It would mean so much to me if you could come with me. I would prefer not to be alone."

"Of course, of course! Let me just check my schedule and if anything, I will move something around so I can come with you. I would want some-one to be with me too!" She compassionately told me. There were no words to truly describe how much that meant to me that she would be ok with being with me. All these years, feeling like I had no real support or understanding. It was like a soothing balm to my overly frayed nerves regarding this part of my life. And she was there when we both started having sex as young adults. It seemed to make sense to God and The

Universe to also have her there during this part of my sexual journey. Her student schedule allowed her to move some things around so she could accompany me to the appointment. We made plans that I would catch the China-Town bus down to D.C. I would arrive two hours before my appointment. That would give us enough time to meet up, grab a bite and find our way to the office in time and if we were early that would be even better.

Everything went as planned. We arrived at Dr. G's office a few minutes early and were given that time to complete the necessary paperwork. Once finished, we both sat in the waiting room, patiently. Finally, I was called.

"Ms. Janelle, a medical assistant in gray scrubs, called my name, while holding my chart in one hand and the door with the other.

"That's me!" I called out and raised my hand so she could see me. My former roommate and I got up and walked over to her.

"Hi Janelle. How are you?"

"I'm fine, thank you."

"And who is this accompanying you today?" She looked over at my friend.

"Oh! This is my friend. She was my college roommate. I asked her to come with me today. Is that ok?"

"Oh ok, no problem. As long as you are ok with her hearing confidential health information that I or the doctor may ask you."

"Oh yes, that is totally fine." I was relieved. I thought she was about to tell us that my friend couldn't come with me.

"All right ladies, come on in..." She led us both through the door into the suite of exam rooms. There seemed to be four, two on either side of the small corridor and at the end was a closed wooden door with a sign that said Dr. Andrew Goldstein. Presumably that was his office.

"Dr. G would like to see you in his office first."

"Oh ok." We walked into his office and he was sitting behind a large dark wood desk. He was wearing a white lab coat, had light colored hair and was bowing his head over his desk, reading what must have been my chart as we approached. He looked up and smiled kindly as the assistant knocked on his door.

"Dr. G, this is Janelle and her friend and former college roommate."

"Hello!" He said cheerily as he stood up and ushered us in. "Come in, come in! Nice to meet you both! Are you Janelle?" He asked as he extended his arm to shake my hand.

"Yes. Nice to finally meet you!" I said as we shook hands.

"And you then must be the good friend?" He happily said to my friend as he held out his hand to shake hers.

"Yes, that's right!" She smiled back as they shook hands.

"Please, please have a seat." He pointed to the two chairs behind us. And we sat down.

"So, I was just looking over your chart but I would love to hear from you. Tell me about your story. Start from the beginning. When did the symptoms begin?" He folded his hands together on the desk on top of my chart and looked patiently at me. And so, I told him my story. I finally came to an end. He unfolded his hands, leaned back in his chair and took a deep breath.

"Well," he began. "Thank you so much for sharing your story with me." I smiled sheepishly. The thought that someone would thank me for telling my story seemed almost ridiculous. I was so thankful that he took the time to listen! "The good news is, your story is like many I have heard before. Your symptoms started not too long after you started your birth control and you were seen for frequent yeast infections and, oftentimes, your providers noted that they didn't even find any yeast. This is all very common. What has happened, most recently, is the effect of prolonged pain and trauma to the vulva area. In addition, that doctor that you mentioned seeing, Dr. Smith?" I nodded my head in recognition of the other doctor I had previously seen with no success. "Unfortunately, he advised you to do the exact opposite of what you should have done. But we'll get to that in a moment." He leaned forward, placing his hands back on the table momentarily before he reached for a large diagram of the vagina. A diagram I was becoming all too familiar with. "So, this is the vaginal opening," he began. "Going out to in, you have the labia majora, labia minora, the clitoris above and then the vaginal opening." He pointed to each part as he named them.

"Now the tissue that lines the opening between the labia minora and the opening, the vulva, is thinner and membranous. This vulva tissue is derived from embryological tissue and so instead of having just receptors for estrogen, it actually has receptors for both testosterone and estrogen. Now, a small percentage of women, let's say about 5% or so, who take birth control pills will have the side effect of significant testosterone reduction. When testosterone receptors of the vulva do not receive testosterone, because the levels are so low, then the vulva tissue is not healthy and this can cause the vulva tissue to be inflamed, dry or hypersensitive. And thus, cause pain during penetration."

Woa! well that's kind of cool and interesting, my science brain thought. I choose not to show my fascination with the science and instead just nodded my head in understanding.

"So, based on the fact that you started having symptoms after you started taking birth control pills and it hasn't really stopped since then that would be my educated guess as to what is happening. Does that make sense?"

"Yes, yes it does."

"So, we will want you to stop taking the birth control pills *immediately.*"

"Ok, I can do that."

"The other thing that is a side effect of all of this...trauma... is that for the past 5 plus years of your life, every time you have had intercourse and there has been pain, you clenched up as a reflexive and appropriate reaction. Because of this your pelvic floor muscles have been overworked and are now dysfunctional, since they contracted too much because of the reflexive clenching. This type of dysfunctional pelvic floor muscles will also cause pain. So, we will need to rehabilitate on all levels at the same time. You will immediately stop taking the birth control pills and eventually, naturally, your testosterone levels will rise back to normal. I will, in the meantime, prescribe for you a gel that is made up of the correct amount of testosterone and estrogen. You will need to apply a thin layer of this gel to your vulva twice a day for the next month. For the month after that you will then do that once a day and so on. And on top of all of that you will need to start seeing a special physical therapist who deals with dysfunctional pelvic floor muscles to help you get them back into their natural relaxed state."

"So, you mean what I did with Dr. Smith possibly made things worse, because he was getting me to continue to contract the pelvic floor muscles?" I asked in disbelief, shock and teetering in anger.

"I am afraid the answer is yes, unfortunately. He may have set you back in your healing."

I looked at my friend and she looked at me. She looked concerned but I was all at once, embarrassed that I believed Dr. Smith, dismayed that I had wasted all of that time and angry about the wasted money.

"Don't get too upset. Unfortunately, this happens a lot with women with vulvodynia. They get told a lot of things that either are untrue about their condition, like "it's in your head," or are given treatment that is counterproductive, like in your case."

"Yes, that's exactly what happened to me." I said, now frowning.

"But the good news is, you found me. And we can help you. You *can* get better. This is *not* going to be how you feel about sex forever."

I nodded my head in understanding. This was definitely hopeful news.

"Now to prove my hypothesis, we are going to do two things today. First, we are going to take your blood to check your testosterone levels, to prove that they are, in fact, low. The second thing we are going to do is to do a physical exam where I administer the 'Q-tip test'" And he held up a Q-tip in his fingers.

"Oh, ok..."

"So, I will do a physical exam to make sure your ovaries and uterus are intact. Then I will place a Q-tip lightly at the bottom left and right, 5 o'clock and 7 o'clock positions on your vulva. For those that have the type of vulvodynia that we just went over, the type caused by birth control pills, the pain is almost always at 5 and 7 o'clock."

"Oh, ok. Well, that is where I have felt pain in the past, now that you mention it."

"Ok, good. So, this will just make it conclusive. So, what you will do is go into the exam room and first do the Q-tip test, then get your blood drawn. My assistant will take you back to the exam room and get you prepared for the exam. I will be there shortly."

"Ok, got it."

The pelvic exam was quick.

"Ok, your ovaries and uterus are good." He said as he finished. "Now the Q-tip test."

"I nodded." My friend gave my hand a little quick squeeze.

"Ok, here we go." He bent back down and a second later I felt a hot piercing pain on the right bottom side of my vulva. The 7 o'clock. "Ok, so I am touching the 7 o'clock area. Tell me what does it feel like?"

"It feels like a sharp piercing pain." I said, trying to be as specific as possible. This really did hurt.

"Ok, just a little more. Now I'm going to test the 5 o'clock area." And just as quickly he moved the Q-tip and placed it on the other side. "What does that feel like?"

This time the pain was much sharper!

"It feels like you're stabbing me with a knife!" I exclaimed.

"Wow!" He responded. "And you see that it's just a Q-tip, right?"

"Yes!" I said in a little bit of shock. He was right. I couldn't believe a Q-tip was causing the pain I was currently feeling on my vulva. If I wasn't the one feeling the pain, I wouldn't believe it myself. He then removed the Q-tip and sat back upright, again, holding the Q-tip in the air with one hand.

"See, and this is just a Q-tip and you feel like it's stabbing you. Now, imagine a penis!" I immediately cringed. The pain I was imagining from a penis already unbearable.

"Ok, well, that is proof for my hypothesis. Let's have you get your blood drawn to test your testosterone levels and then you can come back to my office.

Back in his office Dr. G sat at his desk again.

"Well, as suspected you had pain at 5 and 7 o'clock which is indicative of vulvodynia caused by birth control pills. We will get the results back from your blood test in about a week and we can confirm the low testosterone levels as well."

"Ok," I nodded my head.

"Ok, as for your treatment. Number one, stop taking your birth control pills! In fact, you can never take any form of birth control that has hormones anymore, ever again."

"Ok, I can do that."

"Next, you need to stop having sex. Tell your husband that this is part of your treatment. You cannot have sex again until you are better. Because if you clench up again you are just going to regress and almost have to start all over again."

"Oh! Ok." A worried look was surely on my face. Another difficult conversation to have.

"You're going to have to find alternative ways to be intimate. There are plenty of other things that you can do. I will have my assistant give you some articles and books to read to help."

"Ok, thanks." That would be helpful.

"And I am going to give you the names of a few special physical therapists up there in New York City who will help you with your dysfunctional pelvic floor muscles."

"Ok, that would be great."

"Ok, and here's the other thing. You *have* to do *everything* we (the physical therapists and I) tell you to do. And your husband *has* to see you doing it."

"Oh..." I responded. I raised my eyebrows.

Dr. G explained that men are not as evolved as women and the way that they show their emotions is through sex. Women are much more evolved and can show it through many other means. But men, and he included himself, just aren't that advanced biologically. So, if my husband doesn't see me doing *everything* I need to do, then to him that means that I don't care about him and I don't love him." I was shocked and a bit overwhelmed by this news. It must have come across my face because he continued, "So this is very important that you do *everything*. And he must *see* you doing everything we tell you to do"

"Ok."

"Well, that's not to say that this will not cause any problems in your relationship. What I have found is that vulvodynia doesn't cause the problems, it just puts a magnifying glass on the problems that already exist."

I nodded.

"So, I have seen many couples survive because they have a strong foundation. I have also seen other couples not make it because the other problems are now just out in the open and fully on the surface. I hope that you two are the former and not the latter. But in order to help that along, as I said, you *have* to follow everything I say to do and he has to see you making efforts."

No one had ever explained that to me before. No man had ever been so honest before about the male psyche.

It is not until much later that I would be introduced to many other relationship experts who made 2 things very clear.

1. Men need sex. They don't want sex. They **need** sex. So, women, in relationships will need to make themselves feel sexual more times than they naturally have the inclination to. This will make men feel loved, desired and connected.
2. Women need to talk. They don't want to talk. They **need** to talk. So men, in relationships, will need to talk more than they naturally feel inclined to do. This will make a woman feel loved, desired and connected.

What's amazing is that if women act more sexually and ultimately have more sex with their man, the man will be more inclined to talk to his woman. And if men talked more with their women the woman will be more inclined to have sex. It doesn't matter how things get off track, the minute one or the other gives a little more effort on their side, the other side will typically also do more of what takes them more effort. The most important thing is for both sides to be aware of this, about the other. In this way, they can both work on either making themselves more available for sex or listening more when she speaks and, just as important, they should each acknowledge the other's efforts in their respective areas of effort.

Thank you, Dr. G! I will always be eternally grateful to him, not just for his diagnosis, but also for his kind words of wisdom. Nevertheless, in that very moment, while sitting in his office, it was clear to me that my marriage was one of the ones with the magnifying glass over it. And whatever problems may have seemed like the size of peas before were now the size of watermelons. *But hopefully,* I thought, *if I can show that I am working on it, then things will get better...*

I was wrong.

Chapter 7: "If your compassion doesn't include yourself, it is incomplete." - Jack Kornfield

I recovered. I put on the gel as prescribed, (I may have missed a few days), but I pressed on. I went to physical therapy. It was painful and embarrassing. But I pressed on. I tried to be intimate with my husband in as many other ways as possible, but it didn't work. I pressed on. And one day I finally got to the point where I didn't feel the pain anymore and it was great. On the last day of my physical therapy, I asked my physical therapist: "Will it ever happen again? Will I ever feel the pain again?"

"Well, you may. But the way I look at it, it's like a window. You can open a window and eventually it may close. But you can always go back to the window and open it again. That's what it's like for you. Your pelvic floor muscles may get out-of-whack again, like the window shutting. But now, you have the tools. You know the exercises. You know what to do and how to get the muscles to go back to normal. You have the tools to open the window back up."

"Oooh ok."

"Plus, you will have my number if you have any questions, you just give me a call."

"Ok." I felt relieved by her answer. She was right, I had all the tools. I knew what to do. And I did. I got better. Today, I can say that I don't worry about it anymore.

My husband saw my efforts. He probably thought that I wasn't trying hard enough. Or he thought that my progress was too slow. Either way, he had previously begun and continued to look elsewhere to get the sexual attention he needed. I am assuming, he probably felt trapped in a marriage where he was going to never be able to get what he needed sexually, notwithstanding that I was working on it. In his mind he probably thought that he wasn't getting what he needed. All of this triggered and contributed to my shame-based thoughts. For me this entire situation was evidence that I wasn't enough. That I was defective, even though I was trying. More importantly, the fact that I even *had to* do all of the things prescribed to me by the doctor, only proved that I was defective. I was not worthy to be loved.

The very last time I wore lingerie for him, his face contorted as he looked me straight in the face to tell me, "When you wear that kind of stuff, it disgusts me."

I internalized that to mean: *I disgust him.*

I felt like I was a horrible wife. I couldn't do the thing a wife is supposed to be able to do, have sex with her husband. The way he shows intimacy and creates connection with his wife. Kind reader, you may be thinking that wives are so much more than just sex. But that is definitely one of the more important and basic aspects. A wife is *the* woman that the husband has sex with. The Old Testament describes the act of having sex with a woman as being the marriage ceremony itself. Once the two had sex that meant they were married. It doesn't get any clearer than that to make certain of the importance of sex to a marriage. And I was failing at providing this for him.

How could a husband love a wife he couldn't have sex with? My body failed me. *I failed at being a wife.* The other aspects of who I was as a person, didn't matter. *I was not enough. I was not enough to be loved.*

My self-talk was constantly replaying: *Who could love a wife who couldn't provide sexual intimacy with her husband. Who would want to be faithful to me when I am not loveable? I'm defective. Something is wrong with me. I am just wrong.* My friends couldn't understand what I was going through. Their sex lives were just fine. I felt isolated and alone. These thoughts led to future ideas of what I thought of myself: *Who would ever love me? Who would ever desire me or find me attractive?* The answer I told myself was *no one. If any man knew the real me, the girl who is sexually defective, they would run away from me. They wouldn't want anything to do with me.* It didn't matter that I healed and that I didn't have the pain anymore. My husband showed me it wasn't enough for him. Therefore, I interpreted that as: *It's not enough for anyone.*

So, while I was physically healing my body, emotionally, I continued to have shameful experiences at home. These shame thoughts had almost become like scripts or songs that I would subconsciously recite to myself over and over. Fast forward, years later, they never fully left my subconscious mind. And over time different things would trigger these thoughts. I just wasn't aware of the triggers.

In the future when men did express that they found me attractive, it almost always surprised me because I knew the *real* truth: *I was not attractive to anyone. I was not pretty. I was disgusting. And when they found out the truth that there was a time that I couldn't do things sexually, they would run away. They wouldn't say nice things. And they definitely wouldn't express that they were attracted to me.*

I didn't know the reverse could be true, because I had yet to experience it for myself.

So anytime anyone did express attraction, it was almost like I wanted to prove that they didn't really mean it. Prove my inner shame-script was right. You could say one of my shame-triggers included just the idea that someone found me attractive. I would go into my script of shame and unworthiness. Wanting to prove to the voice in my head that it was right.

As I look back now, I can see clearly how this time in my marriage triggered my old shame-scripts and shame-based thinking. It triggered them into hyperdrive.

So, no, kind reader, my marriage didn't make it. It was never the same.

Chapter 8: The year I slept with a married man...

It'd been three years since my divorce. I had attempted to block out most of the things my ex-husband had ever said or done to me and thought it was time I tried dating. I used the dating app OK Cupid and dated a handful of men. But the dating scene was so alien to me. I hadn't been single in my 20's so this way of dating was very new to me. Out of the seven or so guys I started to date from the app, one by one they weeded themselves out of my life, until I finally started dating one young man, a pilot, monogamously. But he wanted different things than I did in a relationship, so we didn't work out. It was like we were in a long-distance relationship even though he lived in NY. And he didn't want to talk on the phone when he was away doing an overnight. And having done long distance relationships before, I know that communicating daily is important, to me, for a relationship to work. Also, all he seemed to talk about was his job, which I wasn't that interested in hearing about. And he had an idea that he wanted his future family life to be where his wife would be at home waiting for him at the door each time to greet him, somewhere in the suburbs of some other state (not NY). This was the exact opposite of who I was at the time and what I envisioned for my future. I could never see myself leaving New York City and I was definitely not a housewife that would just be waiting for my husband to come home. Since dating didn't work out and was tiring, I started to put more attention into my career and profession instead of focusing on dating. Nine months later, I met a persistent southern gentleman who charmed me with his chivalry, but wasn't the most intelligent. The second time we met and spoke, I lost my voice. He asked if I was drinking lemon juice and honey and I told him I didn't have lemons but I had honey. He promptly went in search of lemons for me. He went off for an hour, apparently going to all of the bodegas in a five block radius and none had lemons, except for the last one he visited. I thought that was extremely considerate. No one had ever gone to that extreme for me before. He would open doors and made sure that I walked through first, he consistently checked in on me, bought me flowers for no reason. However, he had a small vocabulary, couldn't hold interesting conversations, I found myself always needing to explain something to him and he hardly ever taught me anything. But I needed someone in my life who treated me like a queen, even if he wasn't the brightest bulb in the bunch. And so, we became a couple. Probably an odd couple at that. But my internal shame voice reminded me that *I'm not worthy of anything else or better. If I were, I would have had him in my life already.*

On the outside it looked like I was successful to my peers. On the inside I was slowly dying! I was working mostly ten, sometimes twelve and even fourteen hours at work and the money wasn't adding up, nor was my time! It seemed like I didn't have time to do much of anything. And then there was that time I only had $5 in my bank account. I was eating ramen again. I was down to my last can of tuna and pack of crackers. And I just remember thinking: *this is NOT ok. I went to an Ivy League school, graduated in one of the more difficult majors, I had a master's degree, I was supposed to have gotten farther along than this. This can't be it. I can't keep doing this forever. There has got to be a better way!*

The night I was introduced to a unique industry was three days before Christmas. And it was a bitterly cold day in New York City. The Southern gentleman I was dating invited me to a friend of a friend's house that was only a few blocks from my job. They told him he could bring a friend... that friend was me. As I started to walk down the block that the house was located on I remember he called me on my phone.

"Hey are you close by?" He asked.

"Yea I am. I think..." I trailed off.

"Ok good I'm going to come outside and find you." He hung up the phone. Seconds later I saw him speed walking towards me from the middle of the block. He hugged and kissed me in our usual greeting, then put a hand on each of my shoulders, looked me dead in my eyes and said, "They're going to try to sell us something, but we are not buying anything! Ok?" *What a weird thing to say, I thought.*

"Ok yea sure," I responded, "Whatever you want. It's freezing out here! Can we just go inside and get warm?" It was so important to him that we "not buy anything" that he was willing to have this conversation outside where we would almost freeze to death if we stayed out any much longer. His forceful nature, in this moment, is an example of one of the reasons we ended up not working out later.

No one greeted us when we walked in. People were clustered in different corners of the living room in twos or threes, talking amongst themselves. We sat on one side of the couch located in the middle of the room facing a large LCD TV. It definitely felt awkward. After about 30 minutes of awkwardly talking with each other, a pretty young woman, with dark straight hair in a ponytail and olive complexion, wearing workout clothes and a book-bag on her back, came joyfully and loudly through the front door. With a full smile, she yelled to the room full of people "Heeeeey! I'm here! I made it!" There were a few laughs from the group of people behind us. She quickly scampered off to that group of people. These were obviously the people she knew. Quickly a take-out menu was produced as they decided on what food to order. The menu was then passed around for each of us to order as well. I was officially starving by the time they passed the menu to us so we could put in our order. It was for some local seafood takeout restaurant. We called the number at the bottom of the menu and put in our order. It had been an hour since I had walked through the door and still no presentation nor any sign of anyone trying to "sell us something."

Then a few minutes after we put in our order one of the girls from the group behind us stood in front of the room and introduced the person who had come joyfully into the home. She was a personal trainer and managed other personal trainers at an expensive gym chain. Her gym's location was on Wall Street. In the world of genetics and science, where I was from, none of that meant anything to me. But the part of me that remembered my friends from undergrad who worked on Wall Street, thought that saying "Wall Street" must have had some sort of significance, this person might be important, so I might as well listen.

The presentation lasted an hour and twenty minutes. (I later learned that this was way too long for a presentation and the presenter was new). She spoke well and was full of excitement. There was mention of vacations they claimed were really inexpensive, but I couldn't confirm because up until this point, I had never traveled, on my own, outside of visiting my parents in Florida. She also talked about helping people and making money. And not just any kind of money, she talked about passive residual income. And I wondered, how come I had never heard of this type of income before. I went to one of the best schools in the country and it was never mentioned. There was also a possibility, with hard work, she said, that you could become a millionaire. It wasn't a huge possibility but it was way bigger than the possibility I had at becoming a millionaire with the three jobs I currently had, which was ZERO. I had been trying to find a better way to make more money which led me to two more jobs (I was an adjunct professor at two different institutions). I loved teaching but had even less time and I was still just making ends meet. I would think: *This is not right. Something is definitely wrong!* The presenter then went on to say that because of the money she was making with this business, she was able to pay off her $5,000 credit card debt and now worked at her personal training job part time. This didn't seem so bad. I could make money by helping myself and other people go on inexpensive vacations. I had never gone into business before, so I knew nothing about starting my own business. But they said they would help me each step of the way. I wanted to do this! *Sign me up!*

Then she told us it was $375 to get started. I had exactly $420 in my bank account. It would leave me with $45 to my name. And the next morning I was getting on a flight to Florida to be with my family for Christmas. And I still had to buy Christmas gifts for my little cousins. How was I going to make this work?

After the presentation was over. My boyfriend looked at me and said, "I know you don't have the money. We're not going to do this." But that made me bristle a little, because maybe *he* didn't want to do this, but that didn't mean *I* didn't want to. Nor did it mean I absolutely couldn't afford it. Maybe *he* couldn't. Not two seconds after he said that, his friend and the girl who did the presentation came over and asked us if we were ready to get started.

He looked at me and shook his head no. I turned to them and said, "Sorry, I don't have enough money right now."

The girl looked from him to me. Then she said to me, "I totally get that. You would do it if only you had the money, right?"

"Yea, exactly," I responded.

"Yea, I understand." She shook her head sadly and looked down. Then she looked up at me, right into my eyes and said, "But, how long are you going to let $375 stop you from doing what you really want to do in life?"

It was like a punch in the gut. She was absolutely right. My life was crazy. I worked 10-14 hours at my full-time job which didn't pay enough, so I had to get two part time jobs as an adjunct professor at two different colleges. And the money was *still tight! AND she just showed me a way out of my situation! I have to do this.*

"You know what," I started, "You are right." And I got up from the couch and walked to the coat closet that had my coat with my wallet and my debit card in my pocket.

My boyfriend followed me, the entire time saying, "No! What are you doing? Don't do this. You can't do this!" But the more he tried to convince me not to do it, all I kept thinking was *You do not currently pay my bills nor are you going to, so who are you to stop me from doing what I want to do with* my *money?!* He was only making me more sure of what I wanted to do. I came back to the couch, debit card in my hand and enrolled, and got started. The entire time my boyfriend was shaking his head, as if to say, "You're doing a bad thing. You're going to regret this."

But I didn't. And never have. It was the **best** decision I had ever made in my life!

Kind reader, I just want you to understand what I saw when I was introduced to relationship marketing (or network marketing) into my life and I saw a way out. I saw a way to pay my bills and get out of debt. I saw a way to help others and to actually get financially rewarded the more people I helped. And I don't mean in the limiting way of just helping the person or couple sitting across from me at my desk for an appointment, like I did in my genetic counseling profession. I mean helping people figure out a way to make sure they can pay their bills (on time), how they can pay down debt, how they can make extra money by working on their own empire and fulfilling their own dreams and helping others do the same instead of just getting the salary while building someone else's dream. Where they pay you just enough so you won't leave and you do just enough work, so they won't fire you.

To be clear, I joined and did nothing. It wasn't until mid-January when I got a phone call from my mom telling me that my dad had passed out in the backyard and that they didn't know what was wrong with him. She was currently following behind the ambulance that was taking him to the hospital. I was panicking! I immediately started looking for flights to go down to Florida to be with my family that same day or the next. I couldn't afford the price for the flights. I felt horrible! When it really mattered most, money was restricting me from what was the right thing to do for my family. A few hours later my mother told me that my dad was fine. But I wasn't. A fire had been lit. I thought: *Didn't I join something so that way I could make more money and never have to be in a position like this again?* I called the guy who sponsored me and told him I was ready to really do this and what did I need to do to get this going?

Fast forward six months later. I was excited about life. I had just broken up with the boyfriend who was holding me back. He tried to support me by joining the business but ultimately his jealousy of my long hours building my business, always questioning where I was and who I was with was too much for me to want to stay in the relationship with him. He criticized the way I did things and yet wasn't going very far in terms of his own personal dreams and goals either. I stayed in the relationship with him because he was nice at first. But ultimately, it was the jealousy that made me want to end it. There was no way I could grow my business while he questioned my every move. I realized I wasn't going to change my behavior for him if the behavior was helping my business grow. Also,

I was just hurting him further by staying in the relationship. So, I broke up with him by telling him it wasn't going to work. My relationship marketing business was experiencing a lot of momentum. I spent long nights running around the streets of New York City showing people our service and the possibility of joining the team and starting their own business. All I could think about was how we were finally living out our dreams and going after our goals, not someone else's, like at our 9 to 5 jobs. I was fortunate. Blessed for my 9 to 5, but I knew it wasn't going to give me the life I really wanted.

That year I helped more people than ever before to start their own business and make another stream of income. This was fulfilling and thrilling. But I was beginning to feel lonelier and more isolated, even while having momentum and success. I remember telling my friends one day "I need a superman!" My friends all looked at me in shock and confusion. Their faces read *"how can any man live up to that kind of standard?"* And so, I quickly qualified "I'm running around here saving other people being a superwoman! How on earth can I be with someone who is not doing the same? Or worse, needs saving? I need someone running right alongside me doing the same thing. I need a superman!" This would then be followed by nods of understanding and words of encouragement like, "I hear you, sis! You're right!" And I knew it, in my bones, that my superman was out there. My superman would be entrepreneurial and would understand and help me run my business. He would be focused on helping people and would be just as passionate about it as I was. He would love my intelligence and my ambition. He would see those attributes as attractive. He wouldn't be intimidated by them, because his intelligence and ambition would match mine, or be even greater. He would also be six feet tall and handsome. But in the meantime, while I waited for him to show up, I was alone. And I think anyone who was close to me at that time knew it.

It was the type of alone that you didn't know was there, until it was late at night and you get home and there is no one to talk to, no one to share your joys, triumphs, concerns, happy moments with. You're just all alone in your head. I would ache because of the loneliness. It's really hard to explain. It's like a really heavy blanket that starts to envelope you the more aware you are that you are alone. At first, it's warm and comforting because you only have to deal with yourself. You do what you want, when you want, in your home. You can walk around your home naked. It's comforting and liberating! No one is there to look at you and judge your naked form. And then as the minutes and hours drag on, the loneliness gets wrapped tighter and tighter around you and it starts to get heavy and weigh you down. You can't get away from it. It just sits heavy on you and around you. You can't move without it weighing you down. You try to get out from under its suffocating weight and warmth that is now very uncomfortable. But you can't. It's almost just easier just to sit still, not move, and let it overwhelm you. Stop fighting it. It just is.

On top of all of this, I am a hopeless romantic. I had the idea that my superman was *somewhere out there, I just needed to be ready to receive him,* was my constant belief. My biggest fear was that I would be closed off to the possibility that I would miss the man God sent to me because I was so busy being "picky" or "having high standards". I started to believe that if God put any man in my life, then the reason must be because he is the "Superman" I am looking to fly off into the sunset with! I never imagined that God could put men in my life who would *not* be my superman, in order for me to learn a lesson (or many lessons). That thought had never occurred to me.

Eight months after starting my business I was receiving a passive residual monthly income that was large enough to allow me to quit one of my adjunct professor jobs. Eight months later I hit a new level in the company and my monthly income increased. This allowed me to leave the full-time job where I worked ten to fourteen hours per day to take a full-time position at a college. I became an assistant program director of a graduate program. It paid less than the 10-14 hour full-time job, but with the money I was making from my business, I had *options!* I had the option of changing positions to a full-time job that didn't pay me as much, but I could afford to work there because of the money I was making with my business. This was a job that would have better hours and people I enjoyed working with. Also, I had now been on five vacations since I got started. So I knew the vacations were real and amazing!

So, there I was, my business was thriving, yet I was very alone. They say that to be a leader is to be alone, and I could definitely relate to that. But the thing that was tripping me up is that I kept meeting all of these other successful couples in my business. They admitted that it may have been hard in the beginning, but that once they figured out how to use each other's strengths, they had a very strong working dynamic. If one person's strength was to meet new people and recruit, the other one was good at building leaders and creating a strong and loyal team. If one was good at presentations and showing what we have, the other was good at understanding the back office and giving direction for what the next steps were. There were also some couples who built their own businesses separately from each other, but supported each other anyway. Alternatively, there were also some couples where the wife took care of all of the household duties, while the husband was out for hours and until late at night showing the presentation and helping people get started in the business. If it wasn't for those women taking care of the household, the husbands wouldn't be able to go out and work the business for so many hours. I longed for that. I longed to work with someone whose strengths were my weaknesses and vice versa. Then it wouldn't be so hard! I wouldn't have to do everything *myself.* I would be part of a team! I would be a part of something bigger than just myself. The loneliness was one part. The more complicated emotion that I carried with me often at this point in my life was a mix between exhaustion and wanting to be part of a team, a couple. Both of those combined with loneliness. If there is one word that can describe all of that, then that is where I was emotionally. And so... I was open. Open to the idea of inviting companionship into my life.

And then the married man entered stage right. He had known me for three years, had never flirted with me during those three years, I thought we were just friends. He had seen my growth as a person as well as the growth in my business. He wanted to help. And then that night arrived. The night when I was open. Looking back, I have no doubt he felt several of the emotions I just described. The basic idea of him might give me all of those things I yearned for: help when I felt exhausted, being a part of a team, something bigger than myself, someone I could share my thoughts and feelings with, someone who could satisfy the loneliness. No doubt, giving off the energy that I was lonely and looking for someone. And that evening and moment, he was probably reading my energy better than I realized.

He said all the right things to make me feel like, maybe it would be ok. Suggesting that we would be right for each other and that it would be ok if we were more than just friends. Which had me begin to think: *Wow, he finds me attractive?! I never knew that! But he doesn't know the real me. If he did, he wouldn't say that, would he? Could he be right? I'm curious, would we be good together like he says? I'm tired of being alone. But I'm defective! IF he knew the real me, he wouldn't be interested in me romantically, would he?*

There was never a thought that included *I deserve someone better than a married man. He must not respect me if he thinks he can say these things as if he's not married. What about his wife?!* Someone who was not triggered to think shame-based thoughts (most likely) would have thought these things.

Instead, my thoughts continued to spiral. When you're in shame, isolation is what you want to do, to hide. But as humans we are built for connection so you may eventually reach out for some kind of connection, but to things and people that aren't the best. The limbic brain takes over and you go into flight/fright/freeze/fornicate/forage mode. So, my thoughts lead me to find reasons to support what my limbic brain had just turned on:

Maybe it wouldn't be so bad if I gave in to the curiosity I'm feeling and his sexual overtures? Maybe I won't be alone anymore. Maybe God created this moment for just this purpose, for us to be together...

I could not have been more wrong!

Chapter 9: You did it... what is that awful feeling you have... shame?

There it was. This thing that I had done. And I couldn't tell anyone. What would my friends and family think of me? Would I lose their friendship? Would they be scared that I would try to sleep with their boyfriend or husband? Would I try? How could I have done such a thing? I must be a bad person. I definitely don't deserve to have anything good happen in my life. I am definitely NOT good enough for good things!

How could I have done that?
How could I have done that?
How could I have done that?

That question was playing in a constant loop in my head.

The only person I can turn to is Jesus and God. He died for my sins. Surely God will accept me, right?

Wrong! Why would you think that?!?! You have got to do so much more to prove that you deserve God's love. Or anyone's love for that matter. Your parents would be ashamed of you. Your friends would be ashamed to be your friend. You don't deserve to be around them.

These thoughts were my inner soundtrack. I knew the words so well to this song that they might as well have been carved into my heart. I started to read the Bible more and read devotionals about forgiveness.

That helped some. I logically started to understand that my sins, even the ones I hadn't committed yet, were already forgiven. Trying to understand it emotionally, was almost too much. How could anyone love me that much when I'm such a horrible person?

And then the real questions began to kick in: *How could I, Janelle, do what I did? How could I sleep with a married man? Especially, when I knew what it was like to be the wife of a cheating husband. How could I do that? How could I do that? How could I be the one who did something so awful and potentially hurtful? What's wrong with me?*

Something must be wrong with me! *I am damaged. I am no good.*

Maybe if I get closer to God, I can hide under his protection, so I don't hurt other people or myself anymore?

I'd like to say that I immediately changed and started making only good decisions, the best decisions. Especially, when it comes to men. However, I cannot. I wish it was. Unfortunately, that is not how my story unfolded.

Where my business was concerned, I stopped talking to people who would be good prospects. I isolated myself by no longer working with people on my team who would directly increase my income. I didn't want to be around them. I definitely didn't want to get closer to them. I was scared that they would find out and see me for who I really was: A horrible person who would sleep with a married man. Intellectually, I wanted to find new people to build my business with. People who I could create a new identity with. However, if I'm being honest, I didn't think I deserved a new person's partnership or trust. After the two years of building towards success and a significant income, I watch my business plateau and then my income go backwards all the while believing that I deserved it. Because, my shame-based thinking believed: *I am a bad person and bad people deserve bad things.*

In the following 2 years, I made more bad decisions with men, including falling in love with a man who was emotionally unavailable, because he was having a baby with someone else. I had a couple of meaningless flings and a long-distance relationship where no commitment was made. All of that left me feeling even more unworthy of love. I started to think *"I should just settle for what I don't really want because what and who I really want is already taken and if he is not taken, then I am not good enough for him."* Or was it that my decisions didn't make me feel this way, but I already felt this way and I made decisions that supported my own thoughts. It was like a vicious cycle of self-sabotage and loathing. I deserved to be punished. So, I was punishing myself.

Can you, kind reader, relate to this cycle of feelings? Or am I alone here?

It's a deep dark cycle of emotions that exists just below the surface. To everyone else, things are fine, but I was reeling. Sometimes, I honestly thought I had gotten out of the dark cycle by staying busy, being around positive people, and shifting my focus. There is a saying: who you really are is the person you are when no one is watching. Well, when no one was watching, I was a shame-filled person.

And when you, kind reader, have shame-based thoughts or thinking, maybe it looks, feels and sounds different for you. But this is what it was like for me:

I would wake up in the morning, utterly alone and with a pit in my stomach. Could it have been work related or business related stress? Sure, it could have been an additional factor. But I knew that the main issue was that I was living as an imposter, putting on a mask that told the world I believed that I deserved positive things, but in actuality, behind the mask, I did not feel worthy of anything positive or good coming into my life. I felt the exact opposite. I felt like I deserved any and every *bad* thing that came my way. And so I made bad decisions that basically supported the fact that had been drawn conclusively in my head: that I *am* bad, unworthy, a freak, undesirable and unlovable. And you don't even want to admit it to yourself that you're doing or thinking these things. How can you? Or at least, I know I didn't. Because saying that out loud or consciously would make me feel even worse about myself. *Because only "messed up" people self-sabotage, right? But I am messed up!* And so, the mental cycle continued...

I, eventually, stayed to myself. I wasn't trying to date anyone. I felt fragile, poisonous and lost, all at the same time.

This mental soundtrack was on repeat for a long time... until... a FriendsGiving event.

Chapter 10:
FriendsGiving and
"You need to date
Jesus!"

It was a night I was looking forward to! Hanging out with my closest friends and business partners to just celebrate being together and being thankful. Playing games, laughing, dancing, singing, eating good food. It happens one day a year, the day after Thanksgiving... FriendsGiving!

I arrived at my friend's house in Brooklyn with my freshly made salad in hand (I am a lactose intolerant pescatarian). When I walked in, I immediately felt the good vibes! The air was warm and fragrant, with the good food to come, including honey glazed salmon, potato salad, chicken wings, macaroni salad, cornbread and more. For dessert I was excited to try the chocolate chip cookies and apple pie.

My mouth was watering seconds after I took off my shoes and waddled my way into the living room, salad still in hand. In NYC you take off your shoes before coming into someone's place. Because the streets are so dirty, you inevitably bring that dirt in with you on your shoes. So, taking off your shoes when you enter a friend's home is the polite, and clean, thing to do. Several of my friends were already there, some in the living room, many in the kitchen and around the dining room table where much of the food was displayed. I immediately started greeting my friends and some of their kids in the living room, giving warm hugs and kisses on the cheek. Then I padded my way into the kitchen, where the hosts and more friends were. After many more hugs and cheek kisses, I was finally able to ask: "Anything I can do to help?"

"No J we're almost ready. You can put your salad on the table and open up the hummus for the chips and carrots."

"Ok, no problem." My stomach started grumbling as I put my salad down and stole a few tortilla chips from a bowl on the table, sat down to take in the good music and settle my hungry tummy.

There were drinks on the island counter and one of my friends was starting to mix drinks for people by request. She also had her own favorite cocktail that she was highly recommending people try. I'm not much of a drinker. For me, drinking alcohol usually resulted in my taste buds disagreeing with the bitter drink and then within a few minutes of drinking I get congested and can't breathe. And, neither of these things are enjoyable. So, I never feel like everyone else feels when they drink: free and loose. Plus, I never needed alcohol to feel comfortable enough to dance or talk. Just give me a good beat and I'm on the dance floor and I just love deep conversations!

Not soon after I arrived, one of my closest guy friends showed up with his son, sister and a cousin. He has one of the biggest, warmest hearts of any human I know and everyone knows it! The minute he walks in, he runs around giving everyone big bear hugs. Genuinely making it clear how good it is to see each of us. I am no exception, and anticipate my big hug as he approaches the dining table. After our hug he says to me privately that he brought his cousin along with him and requests that I help his cousin feel welcomed as he is a close cousin who is going through a tough time right now. He wanted to bring him around us, his positive, supportive friends. Well, I couldn't be happier to help out!

"Marco, I want you to meet my friend Janelle, aka the professor! She's like a little sis to me and she also does genetic counseling. I know you are getting trained to be a Nursing Assistant so I am sure you will have things in common to talk about."

"Hi Marco, so nice to meet you. And I love nursing assistants! I work with a few great ones. I also teach some nursing assistant students about genetics."

"Oh, really! That's awesome! Nice to meet you. ``We gave each other a quick hug (I'm a hugger). "So where do you teach nursing assistant students?" he continued.

"Oh, I have taught NA students at York College." I answered.

"Oh cool! I am being trained at NYU."

"Oh! That's awesome."

"There aren't that many people of color in our fields are there?" He asked.

"No, you're right there aren't!"

"You should post about your field and get some of your students to post on this IG group I follow. It's called: Brown and in medicine. Lots of people, who are thinking of going into allied health fields, follow it and use it to get info about different career paths. You guys should definitely be represented!"

"That's a great idea! I will follow them now." I took out my phone and immediately went to my Instagram app and looked for the group that he mentioned and followed them as well as liking a few of their posts.

"So where do you live?" I asked him. When getting to know people I always ask where they live, what they do (I already knew that about him) and about their family. I learned this from a book I read, "How to Win Friends and Influence People" by Dale Carnegie.

"Oh, I live here in Brooklyn to be close to campus for school. But my wife and kids live in New Jersey."

"Oh man! So, you are doing a long-distance relationship. What's that like?"

"It's hard! I keep trying to convince my wife to move here so we can be closer. But she doesn't want to take the kids out of their school. Which I can understand, but it would be a lot better if we could be together. Easier for her and for me. I miss them! That's why my cousin brought me to this FriendsGiving so I wouldn't be home alone by myself, missing all my family."

"Well, you have a great cousin! I'm glad he thought of that. We love him and anyone in his family immediately becomes a part of our family!"

"Well, that's great to hear! So, how did you and my cousin meet?"

"We're in the same network marketing business. He has taught me a lot!"

"Oh that's great. Yes, I know several people who are in the same company. It's a great company! Do you know Tim and Sarah Burns?"

"The names sound vaguely familiar..."

"Well they're big time in the company. I am sure if you saw their faces you would know them. They prospected me a long time ago. I was a part of Amway a few years ago and was very successful. I brought in $5,000 a month. So, I know they wanted me to be a part of their organization."

"Yea, I can imagine! So, if you saw the information, why didn't you get started with them?"

"Well, two reasons. One, if I were to get started I would do it with my cousin and two because I am focused on NA school right now and don't want to commit my time and energy anywhere else, right now, you know?"

"Oh ok, I can understand that." I responded.

Just at that moment our host yelled out to the room, "Who is ready to eat?!" Lots of 'yes's" were heard throughout. "Ok great! I'm gonna need the PK to say the grace." PK is short for "Preacher's Kid" and my friend and host was referring to one of our other friends among the group who is well known for being a preacher's kid. But just then Marco looks up in surprise and yells out from where we are across the room, "How did you know I was a PK? Is it something about the way I look?" His cousin is the first to laugh, followed by the rest of the room of friends. Our friend Tom, who was our resident PK, looks up and yells back across the room.

"You're a PK too?!"

"Yea, man!" says Marco.

"Well, you know, us PKs have a certain swag about us. We gotta stick together!" and Tom brushes his shoulders to show us how cool he is. Again, more laughter in the room.

Still laughing, Marco asks, "What's your name, bro?"

"I'm Tom. What's yours?"

"I'm Marco. Well, since you are the resident PK in the room, I'll let you do the honors and say grace." There were smiles and head nods all around. Marco may not have known it yet, but for our room of friends, he just officially became a part of the family!

"All right everyone, please bow your heads..." we all complied, and Tom went into his prayer "Father God, we want to thank you for life today. We want to especially thank you for this unique gathering of friends now all turned family! Help us continue to grow stronger together with you always in our midst. Bless the hands that produced the food and bless the hands that prepared the food. And may it nourish our bodies and keep us healthy. In Jesus' precious name, Amen."

"AMEN!" said the room collectively.

And we all began to form a line to grab a plate and fill our plates with food.

After getting our food and settling back in our chairs, I couldn't wait to find out more about the new member of the family, Marco. *He's a preacher's kid!* I thought. *So fascinating! I am on my own journey to get closer to God. I would love to hear more about that part of his life.*

After about eating half of the food on my plate I finally said, "So, you're a PK huh?"

"Yea! That was so crazy! When your friend asked for a PK to say the grace, I really was shocked. I literally said to myself, how in the world does he know?! Is there something on my forehead that says that?!"

We both laughed.

"Well, usually it's the PK's who are the worst kids, right?"

"This is true. We have been known to get into some trouble." He teased. "At first I wanted to be as far away from the church as possible! But then I ended up playing the guitar for a Christian Rock band."

"You did? No way! What was that experience like?"

"Oh, it was crazy! Those Christian Rock bands live just like the non-Christian rock bands. It's very 'rock and roll.'" I looked at him in shock, eyes wide and mouth slightly open. "Yeah, it's true! They do a lot of non-Christian things. The drugs, alcohol, the groupies... it's all there too! It's ultimately one of the reasons why I left."

"Really?! I am so shocked! I thought they would at least lead a different lifestyle."

"Yea, most people think so, but those in the industry know the truth!"

"Wow!"

"In fact it was while I was on tour that I had a fight with God. That's when I actually got close to Him and it was my reason for leaving. You ever have a fight with God?"

"Uhm no..." again my eyes were wide in shock.

"Yea, well, I did. I was angry with him. I was angry that I was out there doing this music thing, but I wasn't happy! I was mad. I wanted something more, something different. I remember throwing around some things in my room and yelling at him! Even cursing at him. And then all of a sudden, a force just knocked me down flat on my ass. I was lying on the floor and there was God holding me down. And I was struggling! I was struggling to get up but he just held me down. And we were fighting! I was yelling... Yea, it was all crazy!"

"Oh wow! So, what happened? How did you finally get up?"

"I was yelling at him, telling him I wanted to stay in the band. He was telling me saying, 'no you have to leave the band. I am not letting you up until you decide you will leave the band.' And I was wrestling with him for what seemed like hours! I was sweating and my muscles were sore. And then finally he put a vision in my mind of what would happen if I stayed. And I was terrified! It was awful! And then I finally said, 'Ok I will leave the band.' Right then and there He let me up. I stood up, brushed myself off and left the band that same night."

"Wow! That is... amazing!" I was struggling to come up with a word to describe it. 'Amazing' was the best I could come up with.

"Yea it's a crazy story to tell! I know it sounds crazy when I tell it. But it really happened! God saved me that day from a life that could have led me down a really bad path. It's one of the reasons why I want to be an NA. So, I can give back to God's people. Help people in a real way. In a way I wasn't able to when I was in the band."

"I get that! That makes sense to me. Especially the helping-people part."

"Yea, not too long after that I met my wife. I knew she was going to be my wife the first day I met her. Again, I could feel God telling me and pushing me towards her. Because of that we did things the "right" way."

He put his fingers up and made air quotes, for the word 'right;. "No sex, while dating. We waited until we got married. Which, besides getting married and leaving the band, is the third best decision that I ever made."

"Really?!"

"Yes, absolutely. It wasn't always easy, but I am so glad that we did."

"I read a book recently called "The Wait" that basically says the same thing," I said.

"You know when I was working with some of the youth in our church, I remember talking with the girls about that, the importance of waiting. You know one thing that I told them..." Marco trailed off into silence. I wasn't sure what happened. I waited for him to speak again for what seemed like a long time, but he didn't say anything. So, I interrupted his thoughts.

"Hey are you ok?"

"Yea, sorry. Yes, I am. I don't know if this is going to seem strange to you, but it's something that God is telling me to tell you right now. It's something that I told those girls..."

I nodded my head for him to go on... as if he needed my permission when he just got an order from God?!

"You need to date Jesus," he continued, "You need to date Jesus. Get to know him. What he likes, what he doesn't like. How he treats you as well as how he doesn't treat you. Janelle, Jesus wants you to know that you will know who your soulmate is because you will know me (Jesus) in him. You will feel me (Jesus) in him, radiating out of him."

He paused.

"Is this making any sense?"

All I could do was nod my head yes. I was stunned into silence. What he just said scared me, but made total sense. *I need to date Jesus!*

He began to eat more food on his plate while I continued in my stunned silence. And all I kept thinking was *wow, thank you God for sending this man to tell me this message. I think I can do this. I know I can do this! This makes sense. I am always trying to figure out who God has sent to be my husband. How will I know him? This is the answer: I will know him because I will recognize Jesus in him. I will know him because he will want to protect me, like Jesus would. He will want to keep me safe, like Jesus would. He will love me without being scared that my ambition will make him look small. He will love me for me and won't be scared.* A few bites and a few more sips of his water later, Marco finally started speaking again,

"You know, sorry about that if I freaked you out. You know, sometimes God will say things to me that I am sure will freak people out, but you know... I just have to tell people anyway. And I got a very clear message to say what I said to you. Anyway, when I told that to the girls I was working with, they also thought it was weird." I started to laugh. I got a picture in my head of teenage girls hearing the same message and thinking that Marco had lost his mind. The funny image got me out of my rapid internal thinking and I finally was able to speak.

"No, thank you for telling me what you told me." I finally said. "Date Jesus. It's a pretty powerful message. But it makes total sense. I'm so glad that you shared it with me."

"Oh good! I'm glad it made sense to you. Because those girls definitely laughed at me and thought I was weird!" We both laughed.

The party went on that night. My friend Jay was glad that I made friends with his cousin and thanked me for making him feel welcome. But I knew that I should be thankful that he thought of bringing his cousin, Marco. His cousin just passed on a message from God that I knew was going to change my life forever.

Chapter 11: What's it like to date Jesus?

After that party I couldn't get it out of my mind. I made a commitment. I was dating Jesus. If any guy asked me if I was single, I told him, "No, I'm dating Jesus." I told a few of my girlfriends. I am sure they thought I was crazy. A few, maybe felt envious. What girl wouldn't want a message directly from God?! Some direction! Oftentimes I have heard God, but it is not a loud voice. And I definitely have not had a physical fight with God like Marco described he had. I have to admit, a part of me was jealous when he told me that he had fought with God. Although it was a literal struggle with Him, it was also a closeness that I craved and knew I did not have. In church sermons and in the New Testament it's clear that God is a God of love. He loves and wants to protect us, keep us safe. But as humans we have the choice to do as He suggests or even commands of us, or decline and refuse to do it. It's a choice. The great choice. A constant moment by moment choice.

I will be the first to tell you that I do not always make the best decisions. But I claim them all. Good decisions and bad, they are all *my* decisions. I take that responsibility. It's how you move on from the bad decisions. It's deciding you're going to *learn* something from the bad decisions instead of replaying the bad decision over and over in your head. So, I was ready to move on from replaying my mistakes in my head. I was ready to date Jesus.

When I started, I decided I would date Jesus at night, when I would lie down in bed and, typically, felt the loneliest. I would imagine that Jesus was lying down next to me. Holding me in his arms. My head on his chest. I could feel his peaceful, loving comfort and protection surrounding me. He knows me fully, knows all my flaws, knows where all the random, embarrassing body hairs are growing, he knows all about my bad and sometimes horrible past decisions, all the pimples on my face, yet he holds me and he loves me. That's what would calm me down, calm me down and stop me from thinking and re-thinking about the past. I would just fall asleep embraced in the love of the guy I was dating... Jesus.

During the weekends I would salsa dance with Jesus. One of my favorite activities! I would blast the salsa music. Some good classic salsa... Hector Lavoe, Ruben Blades, Willie Colon... And I would dance with Jesus in my living room. (We dance salsa "on 2" of course... only my fellow salseros will understand that). Sometimes the music was so fast we would get off beat and giggle until we found it again. Other times it was slower and sensual. He would pull me closer and we would dance chest to chest. Either way we would always end it with me sweating (salsa dancing is *always* a good workout) and relaxing on the couch. Him next to me. That sweet high of endorphins running through my body and the confidence to know that everything is going to be ok because I'm with Jesus. How could my life not be ok, after a round of salsa dancing?!

Other times I would cook, and He would be behind me sometimes watching me. Not saying anything, just being present so I could feel His strong, calming energy. I would eat and He would be there next to me, just being loving. I would walk my dog and He would walk next to me. Just as happy as I am to see my dog so happy on her walk. We both enjoyed the simplicity of just watching her as she excitedly smelled every new and old scent along the way.

On one of those walks it became clear to me a way in which God treats us like our pets (or dogs to be more specific). I let Bella, my dog, do whatever she wants to do as long as she stays on the sidewalk. She tries at times to just run into the street but I don't want her to be hit by a car, so I pull back on her leash and tell her 'no'. It occurred to me that God is like that with us. He allows us to walk in certain areas, to make certain decisions on our own, all in His loving presence. But those times when we want to run into the street, He stops us and tells us 'no,' because He doesn't want us to get hit by cars! (I thought about naming this chapter just that: "God doesn't want us to get hit by cars").

All this time spent with Jesus was helping. I told men who tried to know my dating status that "I am dating Jesus." That quickly turned most of them off. Which was great for me. The way I saw it, that meant Jesus wasn't *in* them, because if they recognized Jesus in themselves, they might recognize that I was already dating them.

Chapter 12: Now for the Cliche: It's a Marathon, Not a Sprint.

While dating Jesus I met many men. However, there was a particular man I met online. Not a dating app, but Facebook. Up until this point, if you would have told me that people meet their future spouses over social media, I would have told you, no way. But here I was.

He was kind and spoke gently to me. He cared about my safety and wanted to protect me if he could. Even though he lived thousands of miles away. He liked that I was entrepreneurial and I loved listening to his ambitious entrepreneurial and political plans as he was a budding local politician. And even from long distance you could tell that he was affectionate and caring, while still very masculine in his boldness and strong desire to protect, not just me, but all others, including friends, family and those who were marginalized in his community. But mostly, he was fiercely protective of his family. He was honest to a fault, not ever uttering a lie. He delighted in being precise actually. He didn't push me to do sexual things but made it very clear how attracted he was to me and eventually after months of talking every day, made it clear that he believed that God brought us together so we could get married and I would be his wife and he would be my husband and we would have one child, a son. He also told me that having a daughter would give him just as much pleasure. For all of these reasons, I believe I saw Jesus inside of him. I believed that God had brought me my husband.

One of the things that I admired most about him, was that when he made plans, I was *in* his plans. Not like, "oh maybe one day I will become senator and it would be nice if we were married and had children." No like: In the next year I plan to do x, y, & z. And six months after that we can get married. I will bring you with me to all of the State events. I know other politicians' wives will love to get to know you. You can tell them about your business, and I'm sure many of them will become your customers. Then we will have one child a year after that and we will move to live closer to the capital. Yea... like these kinds of detailed plans.

There was comfort in his certainty. I felt like my future was safe with him. And even though miles and time zones apart we found a way to talk to each other every day. Many times, we fell asleep while on the phone with each other. Sometimes intentionally wanting to just be "present" while the other one fell asleep. At that time, in those moments, I felt like I was dating Jesus long distance. So, I let it slide when he started to ask where I was, and who I was with, when I was at business meetings or socials. I let it slide when he mentioned that he didn't like it when I posted pictures on social media showing too much skin. I let it slide when we disagreed and he felt like he needed to give me a 45 minute to an hour lecture about how I was wrong and he was right. Well, I didn't really let that slide, rather, I would put myself on mute, in fifteen minute increments, while turning down the volume on the phone so I couldn't hear him talking and I would do something else, so I wouldn't get bored while I waited for him to finish speaking and calm down.

We would pray together; we did premarital counseling. I did a lot of praying, thanking God for putting this man into my life. I started on a journey of gratitude when our infrequent arguments and disagreements started to become more frequent and get more intense. I was thankful to God for putting him in my life and asked God to help change me so I wouldn't feel as bad as I did when the arguments happened. When the arguments got more intense, and I found myself acting in ways that weren't like me - like yelling back at him (I'm not a yeller when it comes to fights). I found myself getting so angry when he judged me for not doing things the way *he* wanted me to do them. And then after I yelled and acted out of character, the shame thoughts came back: *I am a bad person. What's wrong with me? Maybe I deserve this since I'm not good enough to receive better treatment.*

Our final argument was the point of no return. I had recently received a pair of wireless earbuds and I wanted to call him, while using them to see if they worked. He had told me a month or so before that he wanted to get a pair, and I thought that if these worked, I would send them to him.

"Hey! How are you?"

"I'm great, how are you?"

"I'm also doing great, but I don't have a lot of time. I have a meeting I need to attend in the next five minutes. So I'm calling you using the new wireless earbuds I got, to see if they work. Can you hear me ok?"

"Yes, I can. But I don't know if you should send them to me if they are the same manufacturer of the earbuds I got the other day that do not work."

"I know! That's why I am testing these to see if they work before I send them to you. You said you can hear me, can you?" I got up and started moving away from the phone and out of my office to test if he could still hear me when the earbuds and I were far from the cell phone.

"Oh well, yes. But remember the ones I had started to not work when I was far from the phone."

"Yes, I do remember. I just left the phone in my office and I'm now far away from the phone. Can you still hear me?"

"Well yes, but I don't know, Janelle, if you should send these to me..."

"Yes, I know." I cut him off. I didn't have time to go back and forth about this because of my upcoming meeting. I just needed to know if he could hear me and if they worked and then make a decision to send them to him. "That's why I moved far away from the phone to see if they worked. You said you can still hear me now, right? So that must mean that these work." I continued.

"Oh, you are far from the phone? Well, I can't really hear you that well."

"You can't hear me? Just a second ago you said you can."

"Yes, but Janelle, you know how I would feel if you sent this to me and they didn't work. I would be so upset."

"Yes, I understand that. But that is exactly why I am testing them to see if they work. Because if they don't work, I won't send them. But you said you can hear me." I continued to walk a little farther from the phone.

"Yes, I can hear you."

"Ok good, because I'm very far from the phone now."

"Well, no I cannot hear you that well."

"Really?" I'm surprised because he just said he could. I started to walk back closer to my office and the phone.

"Yes, Janelle, I don't know if you should send this to me because if it doesn't work and you spend all the money to send it to me for it not to work, I will be very upset."

At this point I am annoyed because he has repeated himself several times, which makes me think that he is not listening to me, or doesn't care what I am saying. On top of that I am frustrated because I have less than 5 minutes before I have to log onto my meeting. So with a raised voice I responded sharply, "That is exactly why I am testing it! You think I have the money to waste to send you something that doesn't work?! I don't have that kind of money!" For context, dear reader, it would cost between $100-$200 to send these to him. Not a lot of money, but enough money that it could be spent to pay a bill or two rather than pay for shipping.

At this last comment I made, he exploded and screamed back, "Who do you think you're fucking talking to like that?! You don't talk to me like that! What's fucking wrong with you?!"

I'm taken aback by his abrupt change in tone and language, because he was screaming and now also cursing.

"I'm sorry I got loud but I'm frustrated because you're not listening to me. And this phone call was supposed to be a simple test to see if these earbuds work or not before I have my next meeting which starts in like 2 minutes!"

"Janelle, do you know you're on speaker phone?! My whole family can hear you yelling at me." For more context, dear reader, his family speaks Spanish, he is the only one who understands English. So, I know they don't know what I'm saying.

"So take me off speaker phone!" By this time, I am exasperated and incredulous.

"I just did! But you should have seen the way my family was looking at me. They were asking me, who is talking to you like that? Your future wife?!"

"What? But they don't understand English. They don't even know what I'm saying."

"I can't believe you would fucking talk to me like that! You are going to be my future wife and you are talking to me in that way. Fuck you! Don't fucking try me..."

At this point I tuned out. I was done. I took out the earbuds from my ears. I could still hear his voice (although much more softly) from the phone that was now on my desk. But I had to log into a zoom meeting. We had had conversations before with our pre-marital counselor and I understood that to him, hanging up the phone on him would be the biggest sign of disrespect. So, I didn't hang up the phone but I definitely wasn't going to stay on and listen either.

"I have to get to my zoom meeting now," I interjected loudly into the air. I knew that I was loud enough that he could hear me even though the phone was on my desk and not next to my face. But he was still yelling at me, so I am not even certain he heard me. It didn't matter anyway as I was now busy looking in my email calendar for the zoom link to join the meeting.

"Janelle, did you hear what I am saying to you?!" He was still yelling at me "Don't fucking try me! I'm tired of your shit!"

At that, I moved the phone to the other side of the desk that was farther away from me as I entered the zoom meeting, immediately putting myself on mute. I could hear his voice now sounding distant and muffled (because he was not on speaker phone) coming from the phone on the other side of my desk. And every few minutes or so could clearly hear a "fuck you" or "don't fucking try me" which means he was screaming when he said that for me to hear it so clearly. I was very frightened by how quickly this had escalated. I was pretty sure that had he and I been in the same place at the same time when that conversation played out the way it did, he would have hit me. That's how angry and violent he sounded on the phone. A few minutes later the phone call dropped, most likely because of a poor signal. He then continued to call me 5 times in a row and when I didn't pick up because I was in my zoom meeting, I got a stream of text messages from him basically saying what he was saying on the phone but now by text.

I felt a deluge of emotions. Embarrassment and shame in that I was on my zoom meeting and had what now sounded like a maniac on my phone cursing at me. Embarrassed because I believed that God had put this man in my life to be my husband and how was I going to explain his current un-Godly, or even inhumane, behavior towards me, to all the people I said that he was God-sent. And then came the shame: *what's wrong with me? How could I have thought he was God-sent. Or maybe he is God-sent and I deserve this type of treatment? Is it my fault he's acting this way because I shouldn't have raised my voice at him because I know when I do that, he interprets it as if I'm screaming and cursing at him? If only he would have listened to me so he knew that I wasn't trying to send him non-working earbuds. I shouldn't have raised my voice at him. This is what I get....*

And then... something clicked. I remembered feeling like this before. This is how I felt when I was in my marriage: scared, alone/isolated and like I was a bad person, not deserving of any better treatment. And I knew! I knew that this was not it. This was not the Jesus I saw in him when we first met. This was someone or something else and I needed to get away from. I needed to protect myself.

It may have taken me a year and pre-marital counseling to identify all of this but I did! And I called off the wedding and told him I wanted to break up. It wasn't until then that I saw the truth of what was really happening. We were not a good match. And even though I wish I had figured this out earlier, the truth is this relationship got me through the early parts of the pandemic. For what it's worth, I didn't "feel alone," as I had in the past, when he and I were together. And I think if I hadn't been with him, I would have been isolated and even *more* alone during that time of such uncertainty and anxiety. And I recognize that feeling alone is a trigger for making bad decisions. So, perhaps being with him during that time, even though he is not the husband for me, kept me from making even more poor decisions and creating relationships (or getting into a relationship) with someone who was local and yet much worse, or who treated me just as badly as he did but, in person.

I recognized that I was feeling shame and what had triggered me to feel that way. I talked about it with some friends and my pastor. Without knowing it I had taken the steps that help someone create resiliency from shame.

I have to thank God for that little gift of getting me through the early stages of the pandemic, even though it did *not* look like a gift by the time our relationship ended. The other lesson I learned is that I can figure things out! I can identify when my shame thoughts kick in and recognize when something is not good and remove myself from that situation, and more importantly, that relationship. I may not have done it as quickly as I would have liked, but I did, eventually, do it! It didn't take 5+ years as it had with my ex-husband. And thank goodness I was spared the lesson of him being in my living space and living together or near each other. I think it would have been much worse.

So, I give gratitude to God for helping me see the situation for what it was and I am proud of myself for not ignoring the feelings that "something is not right here" and standing up for myself. That just means I will be quicker if/when the next time comes around. And that, my friend and kind reader, is what they call "Progress". I have not reached the pinnacle of life or a perfect-like zen. I am continuing to progress. And if you were looking for a happy ending, this isn't it. Because, this is not the end. My life's journey continues.

Like life, the process of shame resilience is not a sprint. It's a marathon. It may be a cliche saying but that does not mean it is not true. So, this is a reminder to you, my friend, no matter where you are in your journey, don't give up on yourself. You will make progress and that, I have learned, is what really matters.

Part 2

"It is good to have an end to journey toward; but it is the journey that matters, in the end."
– Ernest Hemingway

Chapter 13: The things to look out for: Triggers

I see the triggers now. The signs that I could be on the path to making a bad decision. For me it is the feeling of being alone. Many times, I would work so hard that when I get home, I wouldn't have time to think about the fact that I was alone. I would just crash (usually on the couch... wake up in the middle of the night and then crawl into bed). I did that routinely, not even realizing it helped to keep the feeling of loneliness away. But then there are the nights I come home, and I am utterly alone. And it was in those moments of weakness that the bad decisions were made. I would take the phone call from the guy who is not ready to commit. I would think it's ok to let this person into my life, it felt good for the moment.

That's where dating Jesus comes in. In those moments of loneliness, I picture Jesus in my home with me, talking with me, sleeping next to me at night, sometimes even holding me. It may sound crazy, but that's what I did. Jesus' love was always warm and safe. I didn't have to fear his love or worry that it would one day disappear. I could feel his presence protecting me, keeping me safe.

Through my network marketing company, I gained a LOT of personal development. My company believes that if they help you make money, they should help you to lead others to do the same. So, they provide training to make sure our heads and hearts are in the right place. One of the trainings included the teachings and philosophy of communication and partnership expert, Alison Armstrong. As a reference as to what a big deal Alison Armstrong is, I will say this: many people know Anthony (Tony) Robbins, the outstanding and internationally renowned motivational speaker and life coach. He turns to Alison when he needs expert advice on communication and relationship advice. I highly recommend two of her audio books "The Amazing Development of Men" and "Understanding Women". Both of these helped me in understanding and knowing myself and being able to communicate more effectively. This is important because our relationship with our significant other, partner, spouse is our most crucial relationship in our adult lives and can have a huge impact on how we show up at work, in our businesses and with our friends and family. I learned from Alison that as a woman I have a primal "cave woman" instinct, that, if it goes unidentified, can cause me to make certain decisions unconsciously (and sometimes consciously). For example, the cave woman has a primal instinct to be constantly aware of whether she is in bodily danger or not. If you are a woman reading this, ask yourself, "most of the time, when I am outside of my house by myself, do I think about my surroundings and if I'm in danger?" Men, ask the women in your life the same question. For most, the answer is an overwhelming YES. For men, this can be very surprising as this is something that they hardly ever consider. For most women, everywhere she goes her inner "cave woman" is concerned about the "tiger" that can come out of nowhere and eat her. For that reason, she is looking for a strong man to protect her from the "tiger." She craves protection. When she is with a man, she feels is the one for her, she will feel a sense of protection and safety in his presence (and in his arms). For this reason, many women, including myself, will do things to please a man to make him "happy" so that way he will stay with her, so he can continue to protect her. But what happens when he is the tiger? When he says things to her that are hurtful or painful? Possibly, you can see, kind reader, how this relationship becomes very dysfunctional. She continues to please him (even if it costs her her dignity or self-respect or worst of all, her own life) in order to keep him around so he can protect her. The problem, of course, is that *he* is the tiger. So, who is protecting her from him?

Another thought: *what if we are the tiger?* What happens when I am the tiger, hurting myself by making bad decisions? When I was eating myself with the bad decisions. Where was the man to protect me from myself? A loving man who cares about you will identify that and would actually take efforts to protect you from yourself. Men will protect women they love and/or care for whether or not the woman is pleasing him, because that is the "honorable" thing to do. Meaning they are built to protect so that is what they will do. It does not matter if the women are saying or doing things that please them. If they see danger (a "tiger") they are built to protect those they love and care for. This means even if the "tiger" is the woman. Learning this, is very freeing for me! It allows a man to be a hero. This is how Jesus was for me when we were dating. I didn't have to fear that I didn't please Him, he was always there to love and protect me. But back when I was married, my husband was the tiger and then I joined in and became another tiger, hurting myself with all of my shame-based thinking. And, later, when I was "lonely" without a man, I let my inner tiger eat me alive by making poor decisions, like sleeping with a married man.

If I could go back in time to that old me, I would tell her that she wasn't alone and is never alone. That she has Jesus with her loving her and protecting her. If Janelle back then knew that, she would have known she didn't feel Jesus' love coming from that married man. She wouldn't have felt flattered, she wouldn't have felt lost, curious, lonely. She would have stopped his advances immediately.

What about you, my new friend and kind reader? Has there been anything that you have done in your life that you regret or feel ashamed about? What is it that you have done in your life? Did you steal money from your mother/father/brother/sister/cousin/aunt/uncle? Did you have an abortion? Did you cheat on your spouse? Did you bully someone to make yourself feel better? For any of the men reading, have you ever felt weak or vulnerable? Did you hurt someone? Do you have an addiction? Did you yell at your kids for no reason? Did you try something new and failed? Did you make a racist decision or action? Did you manipulate others to do your bidding so it would make you look good and them look bad? Do you never finish what you start? Do people know you as the guy/gal who never does what they say they're going to do? Did you call your spouse names, curse them out, did you make them feel small, did you hit them? What did you do in your life that you are most ashamed of? That thing that you haven't told anyone, or maybe one person.

It's quite possible that it's the thing that's holding you back. Because you feel like an imposter. If people knew what you were really capable of, or what you did that one time or multiple times in your past, they would not trust you. They would not listen to you. They would not follow you. They would not like you.

To determine if you have had shame-based thoughts, here are some questions to ask yourself, they are adapted from the Shame Indicator Quiz by shame and complex trauma expert Pastor Tim Fletcher:

1. Have you ever had or currently have rigid core beliefs like: I'm a bad person, weak, unlovable, undeserving, inept, unattractive, stupid, powerless?
2. Have you ever found or currently find yourself constantly belittling, discounting, and criticizing yourself and others?
3. Have you ever had or currently have one or more addictions to substances (including fat, sugar, some carbs), activites (work, spending,

gambling, porn, working out), certain relationships (co-dependence) and/or emotional states (excitement, rage, spiritual ecstasy, or sexual arousal and release)?

4. Have you had or do you currently have a general suspicion and mistrust of other people (even and especially when they are trying to be nice). You suspect ulterior motives?

5. Have you had or do you currently have an excessive sensitivity and defensiveness to perceived criticism or rejection?

6. Have you felt or do you currently feel "irrationally" guilty (haven't actually done anything wrong) and/or anxious about earned successes (the imposter syndrome). Feelings of being a fraud or phony?

7. Have you ever found or currently find yourself endlessly focusing on past "mistakes" in private or publicly?

8. Have you ever had or currently have an unreasonable fear of "failing" "losing" or "making mistakes"?

9. Have you ever found or currently find yourself to be a compulsive perfectionist ("I can't help it")?

10. Have you found or currently find yourself compulsively shading the truth or lying directly or by omission, and denying it to avoid expected ridicule, criticism, or disapproval (also a symptom of excessive fears) – because you have been/are afraid of how others will react if you tell the truth?

11. Have you ever or currently have notable self neglect – i.e. resisting or avoiding appropriate medical care: rarely or never seeing a doctor, dentist, gynecologist, or eye specialist for checkups or illnesses; not getting or taking prescribed medications; poor personal hygiene?

12. Have you ever found or currently find yourself avoiding self-assessment for psychological wounds, and/or true personal recovery – living by "that is the past I'm not going to look at it. It doesn't affect me now. I refuse to look at any of that stuff that may have affected me because it's too painful"?

13. Have you ever found or currently find yourself deflecting, discounting and/or rejecting deserved compliments, and "being very hard on myself."?

14. Have you found or currently find yourself chronically giving time and energy to others, and getting little or nothing in return?

15. Are you unable to do this self-love exercise (answer these questions).

16. Have you found or currently find yourself rarely requesting or demanding what you want, or doing so anxiously and expecting rejection, rather than asserting calmly (asking for help creates anxiety for you, so you avoid doing this)?

17. Have you ever found or currently find yourself tolerating and/or justifying a core belief like "I don't deserve or expect success, love, security, comfort, friends and/or nice things" (I think the best I will do is receive a few crumbs of love)?

18. Have you ever found or currently find yourself engaging in self-sabotage – repeatedly "setting yourself up" for failure, disappointment, frustration, and/or losses and feeling or saying "I can't help it" "it doesn't matter," "I don't care," or "I don't deserve it"?

19. Have you ever chosen or are currently choosing a direct-contact human-service profession – ie clergy, counseling, medicine, education (teacher/prof), law enforcement (cop, probation, corrections), consulting, coaching, training, driving public vehicles, customer service, casework – always need to be in a helping role?

20. Have you ever found or currently find yourself frequently reliving traumatic memories from the past that cause shame?

Now, go through and count the number of questions that you answered yes to.

How many do you have?

Most, who have significant shame-based thinking will have 12 or more where they answered yes.

No matter how many of these questions you answered yes or no to, the most IMPORTANT aspect of this exercise is that almost everyone who takes it can relate to having done at least one or two of these things at some point during their lives, even if it's not right now. Shame is a *human* emotion that *all humans* go through. There are different triggers for each person. However, some have deeper "shame-based thinking", as Tim Fletcher calls it, or "low shame resilience", as Brene Brown calls it. The deepest "shame-based thinkers" are those with little to no "shame resilience." Having little to no shame resilience can cause more serious and sometimes dangerous things like depression, addiction and even personality disorders.

So, can we heal from shame and/or increase our shame resilience? I am happy to report that there are a few important steps that many shame experts agree on. They use different words to describe basically the same things. So, I will, in turn, use my own words to describe the steps needed. One of the first things that helped me face the shame, unpack it, begin the healing process and increase my shame resilience, was finally telling someone of my shameful acts. Telling anyone at all, knowing that they may reject me forever, but saying it anyway. That was the first step. No more denial, I need to face it!

I agree with Alison Armstrong's description of overcoming shame. You need to own it! Without justifying your behavior or making up reasons for it. Just own it. The fact that I, that you, kind reader, feel shame is an indication that we have dishonored ourselves of our principles and values. But when you own it and admit that you feel bad about it. This is the first step to reclaiming your honor, because only honorable people would feel bad about doing it. So, there are different ways you can own it. One example is, you can write it down. But the most powerful thing is to *tell* someone. It's best if you can explain to this person that you are about to own something that you feel ashamed about and that they should listen to you own it and ask them to please not tell you why you did what you did or that it's not your fault. This can be very powerful.

One difficulty in this assignment is, whom do you tell? Should it be the closest person to you? Or can it be a total stranger? You decide. However, you must tell someone. I will say this though, if the first person you tell is a stranger, I highly recommend you tell one more person, a person whom you are a little closer to. Someone in your "connection network." A connection network is defined as a small list of people whom you can trust to share your vulnerabilities with, without worrying that they will use any of your vulnerabilities against you later. This is hard because, often times, we feel like "we cannot share ourselves with others if we see ourselves as flawed and unworthy of connection" So, again, this is hard, however, if you really want to move towards healing and increasing your shame resilience, then, I believe, this step is the *most* important.

The first person I told was a guy I dated. Unfortunately, he found out from someone else and wanted to confirm it for himself and so I confirmed and told him. However, even though it was more of a confirmation than a revealing, this was very helpful for me. It was the push I needed to say it out loud. Once I told him, he of course had questions, and I answered them as honestly as I could. Days later, I can honestly say it made us closer. He knew the worst version of myself, but could still see me for who I was in that moment, not the lost, confused, lonely person who had made that decision in the past. This helped me see myself in a new way.

This also led me to the next step towards healing and increasing shame resilience: You have to figure out why. You must ask yourself: *Why did I do that? What was going on with me? What were my triggers that led me to that point? How can I spot these, so I don't get triggered anymore, so I don't end up in that space again?*

For me it was coming to the realization that loneliness is a trigger for me. When I was alone, I would ruminate on past relationships and it typically led me to the same thoughts: *I'm not enough. I'm too fat, too short, too hairy, too ugly. I'm not worthy to be loved. This is why I am alone.* This is when I feel most vulnerable. For me, this is not easy to admit. Who likes to admit that they feel vulnerable? Who likes to feel weak and an easy target to take advantage of? I think of myself as smart and strong. But I am not always strong, and in those moments of weakness I make dumb decisions. Decisions that can hurt me and others around me. There is a saying:

"Hurt people hurt people." If that was too meta for you, it means that people who are hurting, tend to hurt other people. Not necessarily because they want to, but because they can't help it. If all they feel is hurt then it's hard to give anything but pain to others. What's down in the well comes up in the bucket. If the well is full of hurt and pain, that's all that comes up.

So what's your trigger? What's your kryptonite? What's that thing that makes you so vulnerable that your shame-based thoughts go rampant in your head and tend to lead you towards making bad decisions? You become your own self eating-tiger. And it may not be one bad decision. It may be a lot of small decisions made in your weakness that lead up to one bad decision. But it's really important to identify these triggers or vulnerabilities. This will help so you can start to make changes to create steps that can help you when you feel most vulnerable. When we are in shame, we lose hold of our power because we are feeling feel fearful, confused and judged. Making decisions in this state is very difficult because it is hard to see the choices we have. We feel we don't have any. We're in a fog.

By identifying my triggers and vulnerabilities I was able to make changes. When I feel lonely, I can call a friend. When I feel lonely, I can refocus my attention on whom I can help or serve right now. So, I can take the attention off of myself. I recently figured out a trigger for me that I thought was a way to distract myself. I used to watch episodes of the show "Scandal." I thought it was harmless. But looking back, it helped me to subconsciously feel more lonely, especially in the matter of romantic relationships. No bueno.

What are your triggers? What are you doing, kind reader, that could be making the trigger of shame more profound? What can you do differently? Take a moment and think about that.

If you are really serious about figuring this out and making changes towards healing and resilience here is a Trigger identifying exercise created by Brene Brown:

Identifying Shame Triggers Activity:
Shame trigger questions
- I don't want to be seen as _____

- I don't want people to think I'm _____
- I would die if people saw me as_____

The answers are always based on how others may see you and what others would think of you

For all the areas in which you feel shame (body, parenting, sex, finances, age, etc) answer the following:

- I want to be perceived as _____, _____ and _____
- I do not want to be perceived as _____, _____, _____

Next try to understand the source for these triggers (family, media, societal expectations, etc)

1. What do these perceptions mean to me?
2. Why are they so unwanted?
3. Where do the messages that fuel these identities come from?

Remember that resilience requires us to have to figure out what we are thinking and why we are thinking it. It requires us to become more aware of our thoughts and emotions.

For more serious work, I am going to leave some space here for you to write some of your thoughts down. You can write down what you did that makes you feel ashamed and own it here in the pages of this book. You can also start to describe triggers that you identified by answering the questions listed in the activity above.

_____
_____
_____
_____
_____
_____
_____
_____
_____
_____
_____
_____
_____
_____
_____
_____
_____
_____
_____
_____
_____
_____
_____
_____
_____
_____
_____

Now that you have figured out your triggers and how to put yourself in a better position so that you "un-trigger" yourself. You are in a good place. Time to put it into practice.

I started to ask myself who am I now? I started to put these things in practice. Each day got a little better. Each day I felt closer to Jesus. Because you know, "we're dating." Each day, I felt a little better about myself. Because ultimately, the question is: If I were put in the same position that I was in in the past, would anything change? Would I do it again?

There is a notion that you will receive the same test over and over until you learn the lesson.

I think that this is very true. I was faced with new situations where the men were not married, they were very single, but I also knew relationships with them would not go anywhere. And I, now, know my main trigger. When I feel lonely I make stupid decisions. So, one by one, I made better decisions whenever I was lonely and a single guy would try to make his way into my life or more directly said, when he tried to make his way into my bed without committing to be in a relationship with me. I could set boundaries and say: no.

I felt better each day, little by little. I can confidently say that if I were put in the same position today, that I would definitely not sleep with a married man.

Chapter 14 – Face the mirror & Focus on the person you want to be

Tim Fletcher has a great way to describe what it is like to have shame-based thinking for most of your life. I will paraphrase it here:

You know those funny mirrors in fun houses? The ones that make you look all distorted from what you really look like. Well, imagine if you had only one mirror in your home and it was a funny mirror. These funny mirrors work differently than normal mirrors. Instead of showing your true form, 5'8" with a normal build, it showed you as 3 feet tall and 3 feet wide. Now if that is the *only* mirror in your home and the only image of yourself as you grow up, the 3 feet by 3 feet version of you is how you believe you really are. So, when you go to a friend's house with a normal mirror and you see your 5'8" tall and normal build, you think something is wrong with *their* mirror. You don't believe the image you see. This is what it is like to have shame-based thinking or to be in a state of shame. You see yourself as the 3 feet tall 3 feet wide person, the one who is a weirdo, undesirable, unloveable, not enough. So, when someone gives you a compliment or tries to treat you nicely (puts a normal mirror in front of you) it doesn't make sense to you, you reject it as wrong. You may push people away from you who treat you well, because you don't believe that's how a person who is 3 feet by 3 feet should be treated.

If this resonates with you, the solution is to put yourself in front of better (more accurate) mirrors. These accurate mirrors would be your connection network. You have to have a small trusted group of people in your life. These people will provide an empathic environment for you to talk about your shame. They are also the normal mirrors who show you who you really are. Shame cannot survive in the environment of empathy. Empathy is putting yourselves in another one's shoes, seeing life through someone else's lens. When most others don't want to listen, the empathetic person in your connection network will commit to being in this space with you.

The most difficult thing about shame is that it makes us less able to receive (and give) empathy. Shame likes to protect itself. When we are in shame, it feels dangerous to reach out for empathy. When we are in the middle or height of feeling shame, we are more likely to turn to fear, anger and blame when someone reaches out to us to tell us their story. When we are in shame it is difficult to find empathy for others, much less ourselves.

Your connection network, your normal mirrors, will have empathy. That's how you know they can be and will be a part of your connection network, because of the empathy that they are able to provide for you when you share. The amazing part is, you get to give that empathy right back when they share something with you. These individuals are also capable of producing "knowing laughter." Researcher Marky McMillan says, "Laughter is the evidence that the chokehold of shame has been loosened. Knowing laughter is the moment of truth when we know our shame has been transformed. Like empathy it strips shame to the bone. Robs it of its power and forces it from the closet."

It takes time to find these individuals, but they are out there. For this reason, it is important to recognize that it will take courage to test out and create these relationships. Remember, ordinary courage is to tell your story from the heart. To do this you have to be vulnerable. Once you have this awareness, it is common to want to talk to people to create these connections as quickly as possible. But this could also lead to prematurely sharing with someone as well. So, it's ok to take your time. Shame researcher Harriet Warner, says, "when it comes to sharing vulnerabilities it's wise to test whether the other person is worthy of hearing our stories and assess our own level of safety and comfort in sharing sensitive material. We want to trust that the other isn't going to deny and minimize our pain or alternatively over focus on our problem in an unhelpful way. We don't want to be put down, pitied or gossiped about, nor do we want to have sensitive info used against us." After you are vulnerable and share with someone, that person will feel like they can relate to you better, because they have a similar shared experience, and can show empathy.

Here are some questions to determine who should be in your connection network, your normal mirrors:

- Who are the individuals in my life who tend to talk about others behind their backs?_____
- Who reaches out to you with empathy and support? _____

- Who are the individuals/groups in your life who are quick to cast judgment? _____
- When these people/person are struggling with shame issues do you reach out to them with empathy? _____

- When these people/person are struggling with shame do you protect yourself? _____

I avoid people who gossip or are judgmental. They are not in my connection network and I do not reveal myself to them. They cannot be trusted. I may have them in my life but I don't really share too much of myself with them. I save that energy for those who reach out to me for empathy and whom I know share empathy with me in return.

It is also important to have self-empathy. Self-empathy is the ability to recognize your own emotions and feelings. If we make a mistake and our internal voice says something like, "I am so stupid." Or " I am so messed up" we typically tend to do the same thing to others in our lives, when they make mistakes, including: kids, friends, spouse, loved ones, colleagues, etc. Having empathy with ourselves, helps us to have empathy with others.

To be clear, there are some people who are not empathetic when they hear someone describe their shame story, because they feel that the shame is appropriate. They think: "You *should* feel shame." Some might say that these are individuals who believe that there are positive effects of shame. They believe it creates a moral compass for behavior. While this may be true, it is only true for short periods of time. What research has found is that when shame is used, the person experiencing the shame does not actually change their behavior. Thus, it's easy to conclude that shame has no positive aspect. It is only destructive.

To further emphasize this point, Brene Brown cites a study of four hundred kids. In this study the researchers found that shame-prone kids are more likely to use drugs, alcohol and have suicide ideation. Therefore, shame-proneness increases the likelihood of drugs, alcohol and suicide. They found that guilt-prone kids were more likely to go to college and less likely to use drugs, alcohol and suicide ideation. Remember, the difference between shame and guilt: Guilt is "I did something bad"; Shame is "I am bad."

Healing and creating shame resilience requires pivoting from a mindset of perfection to focusing on growth. Remember: we cannot use shame to change. We cannot change and grow when we are in shame. Perfection is not something we can actually attain. It is absolutely impossible for us to do everything that is expected of us or that we expect of ourselves. But starting to have ideas like, "I'd like to get better at this," you actually start with who and where you are. The *real* you. Not the projection of perfection that you keep trying to be. Giving ourselves permission to be imperfect helps us to identify our self worth despite our imperfections. What's even more helpful is when we create connection networks that affirm and value us as imperfect beings. This promotes positive change.

When attempting to attain perfection, those who have little shame resilience view past mistakes and failures as lasting and permanent. This completely alters their access to power and connection. Looking at ourselves and how we can grow, rather than how we can be perfect, allows us to choose empathy and connection with others. Literally we are able to find the kryptonite of shame. There is an acronym for S.H.A.M.E. that stands for Self Hatred At My Expense. When one employs self-acceptance it creates an understanding of self, where we want to go and how we want to get there. This promotes viewing ourselves with compassion, rather than self-loathing. Getting rid of the S.H.A.M.E.

Here is the thing about self-acceptance. It is not a feeling. It is a choice! Many times, I say affirmations (ie: I am beautiful, I am worthy, I am loveable, etc) or I get a compliment saying the same thing but I don't "feel" like any of my affirmations or the compliments. I don't *feel* beautiful. I don't *feel* like I'm worthy. I don't *feel* like I'm loveable. The key is that it is a choice. I have to *choose* to accept myself as who I actually am. The plump, hairy, quirky *and* beautiful *and* imperfectly loveable me. Acceptance is a choice. And you have to keep *choosing* to accept yourself until you believe and *feel* it.

The other healing and shame-resilience tool I started to employ was to focus on the woman I wanted to become. I started focusing on my growth. If I wanted to step into the version of me that was growing, that meant that I would be able to identify my shame triggers and take the steps necessary to move away from them to this would prevent me from making stupid decisions. I started to focus on what that would look like. What does she focus on each day? What does her day look like? What is her routine?

I know I want to be a wife again. I want to be the type of wife who helps her husband in his business and his purpose. Who helps provide solutions when he can't seem to think of any. Who supports his dreams when others say he can't do it or it can't be done. I want the type of husband who can help me in my business, help me with plans and my purpose to help those around the world get through shame and isolation, disconnection and self-sabotage.

If I want to be this type of woman to attract this type of man, what does that mean? What do I have to bring into my life, to be that person now? One thing I did was to be more aware of those who have big ideas to help people around the world. I was always looking for a way to help. I began to think, *how can I help? Whom can I connect them with, if I, personally, can't help? What can I do? How can I serve?*

How can I serve?

You, reader and new friend, how can I serve you? And in turn, whom can you serve?

Chapter 15: Tired of playing small. Go big or Go home!

I imagine we all have something that we regret. Maybe your version of "sleeping with a married man" is that you stole money from your family, or you were the one who cheated on your spouse, or are you a man who was seen as weak, or you had an abortion, or you hit someone in a car accident, or you went to jail for committing a crime, or you never follow through on any of the promises you make, or you never finish what you start, you're a bad father or mother, or you told lies about your best friend... whatever it is, it is something that you believe if people knew, it would change your life for the worst. Well, let me be the first person to tell you. That thing that you did doesn't define who you are. Did you learn from what you did? Have you decided that you will never do that again? Welcome to the new world of self-forgiveness. You have just made the first step.

Learning from our mistakes, bad decisions and failures is how we learn. Ever since we were babies, that is how we learned. When we began to learn how to walk, we saw everyone else around us walking, so we knew it was possible, and we just kept trying. We would fall and learn not to put too much weight in one direction or another and then we fell again and learned a new lesson about how to place our feet and then we fell again and we learned a new lesson about where to put our hands. Think about it, we fell (and failed) more than one hundred or even one thousand times while trying to learn how to walk, but we didn't give up, we kept learning. That is what I am learning about this thing we call life. The shame that surrounds our failures and mistakes is self-imposed. The rest of the world doesn't necessarily see us the way we see ourselves. And if there are people in your life who do make you feel shame over what you have done, who do not give you the room, or space, or grace to learn from your mistake(s), to move on and grow, give yourself permission to remove those people from your life. The reason you are keeping them in your life is probably because they secretly support your own belief that you don't deserve to be forgiven, and that you can't learn and grow. I am not saying this to be mean. I am telling you out of the love I have for you as a fellow human and the desire to see you grow. You have to remove those people from your life and find people who are positive, supportive and push you to look at your flaws and to grow from failures. Find your connection network, your good mirrors.

You are not your past! I am not my past. You are an amazing person who made a bad decision, or did something bad or hurtful, or made a mistake. But you learned from it. You grew from it. That experience helped to make you the person you are today. And people need to hear from you. They need to hear *your* story. They need to know what you did wrong so others don't feel so alone in their isolation. So, they know that someone else made the same mistake and came out of it on the other side, maybe a little scared, but alive and, perhaps, even thriving! But you can't do that in a place of shame. You will remain small and keep your gift to others, hidden. Whom will that inspire? Whom will that help? No one.

I believe we were born to live, learn, love, grow, give, and guide. We are human. Humans are social creatures. When we feel shame and guilt we hide and isolate ourselves. This makes us feel even more alone. I believe this quote sums up one of my deepest beliefs:

> *Our deepest fear is not that we are inadequate. Our deepest fear is that we are powerful beyond measure. It is our light, not our darkness, that most frightens us. We ask ourselves: Who am I to be brilliant, gorgeous, talented, fabulous? Actually, who are you not to be? You are a child of God. Your playing small does not serve the world. There is nothing enlightening about shrinking so that other people won't feel unsure around you. We were born to make manifest the Glory of God that is within us. It is not just in some of us. It is in everyone. As we let our own light shine, we unconsciously give other people permission to do the same. As we are liberated from our own fear, our presence automatically liberates others. - Spiritual Teacher, MaryAnn Williams*

Often, while in shame-based thinking, we go out in the world but we put on mask so people can't see the real us. For this reason, people may think we're happy and we have everything together. The truth is, however, that we are seemingly happy on the outside but living a quiet life of desperation and shame on the inside. This creates a negative shame cycle.

This false image we have created of ourselves makes us feel disingenuous when we go out into the world and meet and talk to other people. This disingenuousness causes us isolate from others even more, in that we don't want to show them too much of who we are. We wear masks and build walls so they can't see us for the shameful person we believe we are deep down on the inside. This is a subtle and painful way to isolate ourselves. Maybe it's a form of self-punishment. Maybe we believe we need to continue to be punished for what we have done in the past. This earlier quote reminds me to ask: how long should that punishment last? And if we punish ourselves into isolation, whom are you helping? The person out there who could be helped and guided by our story is now also left in isolation and hurting. If we muster up ordinary courage, bring down the wall, take away the masks and be vulnerable to share our story, it could be the one thing that helps someone move forward in their own life, and be a little freer from their own shame.

Now I'm not saying that you must write a book and "put your business out there" (as my mother would say). You can start by telling the people in your connection network, your good mirrors, about what you did and sharing how it affected you and what you have learned. Start there. You never know who in your network could learn from you and that may be enough.

So, kind reader, you may be asking: what did *you* learn, Janelle? Great question! I learned a lot. I learned that one of my biggest shame triggers is being alone or feeling lonely and that is when I make my poorest decisions. I learned to stay with friends and people I can trust for as long as I can and to stay as busy as I can so I can fall asleep before even feeling alone. I learned that I can call girlfriends when I feel alone and we can just talk. Maybe they want someone to talk to also. I learned that my own peace is more important than satisfying anyone's curiosity or other desires. I learned that I am stronger than I look. I learned that I am not my past, and I am not my bad decisions and I am not my failures. I learned that my energy is powerful. God decided to put a bright positive energy in me and I have to protect that. If it gets dimmed, then I am damaging the gift that God gave me. God wants me to share that positive energy with others, but it is not easy to do that when I am lost in doubt, shame and fear. If you are waiting for me to say something like "*I learned not to trust men or even I learned I can't trust myself around men,*" I am sorry to disappoint you. I don't believe that all men are bad. I don't believe that all men have an ulterior motive. If I believed that, then I will never find my husband because I will push him away and be closed off to him. Instead, I learned I *can* trust myself around men. I have always been able to. I know how to keep a wall of distance and professionalism. Another important lesson is that not everything is as simple as it once was, and my decisions and actions carry a far greater effect than I allowed myself to acknowledge. There was a fleeting moment when I may have thought my actions or decisions didn't matter so much. I know, now, that I couldn't be more wrong about that. And most importantly, the person who was most affected was *me*. I hurt myself and hurting myself doesn't help anyone.

And just to be completely clear, I learned not to sleep with a married man. I knew that before, but I may have questioned it in a moment of weakness and that will *not* happen again. I thank God for these lessons! I can look back and say that I had to learn these lessons to be a stronger person. To be the person I am today and the person I am becoming. To be able to share my lessons with others, so I can stop dimming my light and let it shine for others. To give hope to others, so that they know that there is something on the other side of shame. There may be a lesson on the other side and dare I say... confidence! The confidence to know that you got through it all and made it to the other side. And maybe the most exciting part is, as it turns out, you are not alone! There are others struggling with shame just like I was, and maybe just like you were or are now. There are others who are looking for a way out and just don't know how to do it. They don't know how to move. They're stuck and alone in their isolation. But we can show them the way to the other side, you and me, kind reader and friend. One person at a time. One soul at a time. One light at a time...

TO BE CONTINUED...

About the Author

Janelle Villiers
Empress Sol Productions

Janelle Villiers is a certified genetic counselor and professor. She has been a relationship marketer for over 7 years. Through her relationship marketing career she was introduced to personal development. It is her unique life experiences in combination with her teaching and personal development exposure that make her distinctly qualified to be able to use her story as a means to help others who are also struggling with similar shame-based challenges she experienced.

Janelle is an avid traveler and can be seen having adventures all over the world. She currently lives in Westchester County in New York with her dog, Bella, enjoying the ultimate adventure: Life. You can follow along in their journey on social media.

www.ingramcontent.com/pod-product-compliance
Lightning Source LLC
Chambersburg PA
CBHW060336130626
46553CB00003B/1019